Miss Polly's KITCHEN

Miss Polly's KITCHEN

FOR THE LOVE OF EATING

POLLY MARKUS

ALLEN&UNWIN
SYDNEY • MELBOURNE • AUCKLAND • LONDON

To my family and friends, and to my mum and my late dad, who taught me the joy of food, family and cooking

Contents

Introduction

I have only a few rules when it comes to cooking:

1. It has to be a good time. If you're not having fun, it's time to put down the pans.
2. Always make enough to have leftovers.
3. Flavour, flavour, flavour.

I started the Instagram account *Miss Polly's Kitchen* in March of 2020 as a place to share recipes with those closest to me. For as long as I can remember, my love of cooking has generously overlapped with my social life. Following al fresco weekend lunches at friends' houses, or Sunday dinners with my extended family, people would often ask how to recreate certain dishes. In essence, *Miss Polly's Kitchen* was a place to document some of the personal recipes I had developed over a lifetime of loving good food and a three-year stint working as a crew chef on a superyacht.

Then, in its unforeseen way, Covid-19 happened. So when my day job as a commercial real estate agent temporarily drew to a halt, I threw my energy into the place that felt most natural — the kitchen. Away from life's normal routine, I had more time to create and share recipes. It just so happened that everyone else had turned to cooking too; they were filling their time with it, including a few friends who were following my account.

I don't quite know what to attribute the uptake to, but I do like to think of the food I create as fairly vibrant and flavourful. It is also colourful, which I hope has a

subliminally uplifting effect on people. During lockdown especially, I think everyone was looking for a departure from their everyday repertoire, but something that was still achievable.

Those who know me best know that one of my biggest fears is the prospect of going hungry. Outrageous, I know. Beyond that, I have a knack for homing in on the one thing I feel like eating at any given time. Generally, I start with a protein — fish, prawns, halloumi, chicken — before deciding on an ethnicity. From there I write down all the flavours and think of how I can magic that up into a dish.

I have a huge love for Asian cuisine; the flavours are so fresh and bold, and fortunately it's a genre that most people love to eat. I'm also big on herbs and adore anything Middle Eastern. The variation of produce used in that style of cooking is inspiring and there is so much depth to the spices at play.

If I have to think of what underpins a perfect dish (or combination of dishes), it is no doubt the social aspect that comes with eating or sharing a meal. Ever since I can remember, my parents have hosted dinner parties and get-togethers at home where there was always an abundance of amazing food, often with a Mediterranean bent. My late father was extremely well travelled and just loved these flavours, and his approach to hospitality was second to none.

Today, my home very much operates with an open-door policy. My friends and family know that I'm never far away from preparing or eating a good meal. Furthermore, I'm a people pleaser *and* a very social person. The real pleasure for me is cooking for others — it's the old cliché of bringing people together. To me, it's the best feeling to be able to take the pressure off everyone in the room by preparing food while everyone else relaxes and, eventually, sitting down together to enjoy it.

Aside from the first few pointers above, I really don't adhere to a rulebook when it comes to cooking, only that it should never be taken too seriously. The head chef who first employed me on the superyachts said that she had never met anyone whose eyes lit up so brightly when they were talking about food, and that is the premise I keep coming back to — pure joy. Most of these recipes have been written with entertaining in mind and are best enjoyed sitting outside with the accompaniment of a lightly chilled rosé or chilli margarita.

For those using this book, my biggest thanks for your support. I hope it equips you with a collection of recipes that you can proudly share with your loved ones. And if you have to undo your top button in the process, well, I approve of that too.

P.S. It might be worth planting a herb garden.

BRUNCH

GRAVLAX SALMON WITH ALL THE TRIMMINGS

I inherited this recipe from my late dad, so I share it with pride. When I was growing up, weekend breakfasts with him would often involve gravlax salmon on toast with a side of extremely buttery scrambled eggs and a glass of fresh orange juice. The beauty of this recipe is in its simplicity, but you do need to plan ahead. Always ask for fresh salmon!

SERVES 4

3 tablespoons coarse sea salt
2 tablespoons soft brown sugar
1 teaspoon cracked pepper
500 g (1 lb 2 oz) side boneless, skinless salmon
¼ cup roughly chopped fresh dill
2 tablespoons gin

TO SERVE

Fresh sourdough – sliced
⅓ cup capers or caperberries
½ cup cream cheese
1 large avocado – flesh sliced
¼ red onion – thinly sliced
A handful of fresh dill or fresh herbs of your choice – roughly chopped
Lemon wedges

Mix the salt, sugar and pepper.

Place the salmon skin-side down on a piece of plastic wrap large enough to wrap the salmon twice.

Pour the salt mixture over the salmon and pat it firmly onto the flesh, including the sides.

Place the dill on top of the salt mixture, then drizzle with the gin.

Tightly wrap the salmon in the plastic wrap. Place it into a dish skin-side up.

You need to weigh the salmon down, so place a slightly smaller dish or a small breadboard on top of the salmon, then top with some bottles of milk or cans to weigh it down.

Place in the fridge for 72 hours. It's okay if some of the liquid seeps out of the plastic wrap.

Unwrap the salmon, scrape the salt mixture into the sink and pat down the salmon using paper towels. Slice as thinly as you can on a slanted angle, arranging the slices on a serving plate.

Get the bread in the toaster. Put the capers and cream cheese in two separate serving ramekins. Arrange on a serving platter with the gravlax, avocado, onion, dill and lemon wedges so everyone can help themselves.

SMOKY CHORIZO BAKED BEANS

For someone who grew up having a strong dislike for beans, I have done a one-eighty in the last few years and now I absolutely love this version of the classic baked beans on toast. This is a hearty and tasty breakfast that easily doubles if you are feeding the masses. You can make it ahead of time and reheat it before serving (add a splash of water if you do this). Serve with toasted sourdough and poached eggs.

SERVES 4

200 g (7 oz) chorizo
    sausages – diced
1 large brown onion – diced
3 garlic cloves – roughly
    chopped
1 tablespoon dried Italian
    herbs
1 teaspoon smoked paprika
400 g (14 oz) can butter
    beans – drained and rinsed
400 g (14 oz) can cherry
    tomatoes
½ cup chopped Italian parsley

TO SERVE

Sourdough – sliced and
    toasted
Poached eggs
Chilli flakes (optional)

Heat a medium pan on medium heat and fry the chorizo for 5 minutes. You don't need to add oil as the fat from the sausage will be enough.

Add the onion and cook for a further 5 minutes. If you feel like the pan is dry add a teaspoon of oil. You don't want to burn the onion, so turn down the heat if required.

Stir in the garlic, Italian herbs and paprika. Add the butter beans and canned tomatoes. Fill the tomato can halfway with water, swirl it around and pour it into the pan.

Season well with salt and cracked pepper, stir and then simmer for 15 minutes.

When the beans have 5 minutes of cooking time remaining, start toasting the bread and poaching the eggs.

Fold the parsley through the beans and serve with the poached eggs on top. If desired, sprinkle with chilli flakes.

ZUCCHINI & PEA FRITTERS

These fritters remind me of summertime at the beach — most definitely with a little too much gin consumed the night before. They are the perfect soaker-upper! A poached egg on the side is a welcome addition, as is a little Kewpie mayo, if you're that way inclined. I like to heat up any leftovers and top them with cream cheese and smoked salmon.

SERVES 4

2 cups grated zucchini (roughly 2 large zucchini)
1 cup peas – defrosted
⅓ cup thinly sliced spring onion
1 cup finely chopped fresh basil
½ cup finely chopped Italian parsley
4 eggs
½ cup grated parmesan
½ teaspoon chilli flakes
Zest of 1 lemon
¾ cup flour
250 g (9 oz) streaky bacon
Oil, for frying

TO SERVE

Beetroot relish
Sour cream
Dukkah
Lemon wedges

Preheat the oven to 120°C (235°F) fan bake.

Lightly salt the grated zucchini. Place it on paper towels, then gently roll it up and squeeze out the liquid.

Transfer to a large mixing bowl. Add the peas, spring onion, basil, parsley, eggs, parmesan, chilli flakes and lemon zest and mix with a large spoon until well combined.

Fold in the flour and season with salt and cracked pepper.

Start frying the bacon in a large pan on a low/medium heat.

Heat a second large pan on a low/medium heat. Add roughly 1 tablespoon of oil to the pan. Spoon ⅓ cup of fritter mixture into the pan and gently press down to slightly flatten. Repeat with more mixture. You should be able to fit 3 fritters in the pan at a time.

Cook for 1–1½ minutes per side. Keep the cooked fritters warm in the oven as you fry another batch.

Serve with the bacon, a spoonful of beetroot relish and sour cream, a sprinkle of dukkah and a wedge of lemon.

BUTTERY NDUJA FRIED EGGS

Nduja is a spicy spreadable salami that can also be used in cooking. This breakfast is bound to impress whoever is lucky enough to be eating in your company. If you're making it for 4 people, double the recipe but be sure to use two separate pans.

SERVES 2

40 g (1½ oz) butter
40 g (1½ oz) nduja
2 slices fresh bread
4 eggs
½ cup thick Greek yoghurt
Juice of ½ a lemon
2 tablespoons grated parmesan
A handful of fresh basil – roughly chopped

Heat a medium non-stick pan on a low heat.

Add the butter and nduja. Using a wooden spoon, carefully press down on the nduja to break up the chunks.

Place the bread in the toaster.

Once the butter begins to lightly sizzle, crack the eggs into the pan.

Mix the yoghurt and lemon juice. Smear over two plates.

Once the bread is toasted, place it gently on top of the yoghurt. Alternatively, you can serve the toast on the side.

When the eggs are nearly cooked, sprinkle the parmesan over the top. Then, once the eggs are cooked to your liking (they only take a few minutes) gently lift them out of the pan and place on the toast or yoghurt.

Drizzle the buttery nduja goodness around the eggs and sprinkle with the basil.

LIGHT
IDEAS

BAKED HERBY EGGPLANT ON A YOGHURT WHIP

This dish was inspired by one of my favourite chefs, Yotam Ottolenghi. I truly adore that man. You can make it ahead of time, then, just before your guests arrive, add the eggplant to the yoghurt. It can be served hot or cold.

**SERVES 6 AS
A STARTER**

2 large eggplants – cut into 2 cm (¾ in) pieces
⅓ cup olive oil
6 garlic cloves – diced
1 tablespoon cumin seeds
½ teaspoon chilli flakes
⅓ cup fresh thyme
⅓ cup fresh oregano (plus extra for garnish)
Zest of 1 lemon
1 cup thick Greek yoghurt
Juice of 1 lemon
A drizzle of balsamic glaze
¼ cup pine nuts – toasted

TO SERVE

Fresh sourdough – sliced – or artisan crackers

Preheat the oven to 190°C (375°F) fan bake.

Place the eggplant on a baking tray, drizzle with the olive oil and sprinkle with the garlic, cumin seeds, chilli flakes, thyme, oregano and lemon zest. Season with salt and cracked pepper and toss to combine.

Bake for 35 minutes or until the eggplant is nice and soft.

When the eggplant is nearly cooked, mix the yoghurt with the lemon juice. Smear it onto the base of a serving platter.

Spoon the eggplant and all its oily goodness on top of the yoghurt.

Lightly drizzle with the balsamic glaze (as you would a salad dressing) and garnish with the remaining oregano and pine nuts. Serve immediately with the sliced fresh sourdough or artisan crackers.

TUNA TONNATO

This is my spin on the Italian classic Vitello Tonnato, which is traditionally made using veal instead of fresh tuna. My old head chef Jen from the yachts introduced me to this dish. I think I was the most untrained crew chef she had ever met, and my god did we laugh. I think my shoddy dance moves made up for my lack of culinary talent at the time; she taught me a lot while I kept the spirits high in our tiny galley. I never tell my guests that there is canned tuna in the sauce — some things are better left unsaid.

**SERVES 4 AS
A STARTER**

3 tablespoons olive oil
¼ cup capers
400 g (14 oz) boneless,
   skinless tuna steak
A big handful of rocket leaves
⅓ cup shaved parmesan

TONNATO SAUCE

95 g (3¼ oz) can tuna in oil
½ cup mayonnaise (I use Best
   Foods)
2 tablespoons capers
2 tablespoons lemon juice

To make the Tonnato Sauce, blitz the ingredients, including the oil from the canned tuna, in a food processor. Season with salt and cracked pepper. Set aside.

Heat a small pan on a medium heat. Add 1 tablespoon of the olive oil. Fry the capers until they are super crispy. Leave to cool on a paper towel.

Heat the remaining 2 tablespoons olive oil in a large pan on a medium/high heat.

Season the tuna steak with salt and cracked pepper. Sear for 45 seconds on each side.

Let the tuna rest for a couple of minutes, then cut against the grain into roughly 1 cm (½ in) slices.

Smear half the Tonnato Sauce onto the base of a serving platter or plates.

Top with the sliced tuna, then drizzle with the remaining sauce. Finish with the rocket, parmesan and crispy capers.

FISH CRUDO

Raw fish is one of my favourite foods in the world — that and oysters. This is a light dish with the perfect balance of zest and a little spice, thanks to the fresh chillies. Serve it alongside some corn chips and wash it down with a margarita and that is what I call heaven!

SERVES 4–6 AS A STARTER

400 g (14 oz) boneless, skinless kingfish
2 baby cucumbers – thinly sliced
1 avocado – flesh thinly sliced
1 blood orange – peeled and segmented
1 orange – peeled and segmented
½ cup roughly chopped fresh dill
½ cup roughly chopped fresh coriander
1 red chilli – thinly sliced
Zest of 1 lime

CITRUS DRESSING

3 tablespoons extra virgin olive oil
1 tablespoon rice wine vinegar
1–2 teaspoons sugar
Juice of ½ an orange
Juice of 2 juicy limes (zest one first for garnish)
1 small shallot – very finely sliced

To make the Citrus Dressing, whisk the olive oil, vinegar, sugar and orange and lime juice in a bowl. Stir in the shallot. Set aside.

Using a sharp knife, cut the kingfish into roughly 1 cm (½ in) slices.

To make the Crudo, scatter the kingfish, cucumber and avocado slices and the orange segments onto a large serving platter or plates.

Give the dressing a good stir, then pour it over the Crudo, evenly distributing the shallot.

Garnish with the dill, coriander, chilli and lime zest and serve immediately.

SALMON TOSTADA

Tostadas are tasty little starters that are always a hit. I ate a lot of these when visiting Tulum, Mexico, along with consuming a lot of tequila. It's a hell of a combo if I say so myself. On that note, look up the Be Tulum playlist on Spotify and play this while prepping — it'll really get you in the mood. There will be enough dressing left over to throw on your next salad too — bonus!

SERVES 4–8

8 mini soft tortillas
500 g (1 lb 2 oz) boneless, skinless salmon
1 avocado – flesh diced
¼ small red onion – finely diced
1 radish – thinly sliced
½ cup roughly chopped fresh coriander
1 red chilli – thinly sliced
1 tablespoon chives – finely chopped

DIJON DRESSING

½ cup olive oil
1 tablespoon Dijon mustard
½ tablespoon red wine vinegar
½ tablespoon sugar

SRIRACHA MAYO

¾ cup mayonnaise (I use Best Foods)
1½ tablespoons sriracha (or more or less, to taste)

Preheat the oven to 180°C (350°F) fan bake.

Lightly spray the tortillas with oil on both sides. Using a fork, pierce a few holes in each. Bake for 5 minutes per side or until crispy. Set aside to cool.

To make the Dijon Dressing, whisk the ingredients in a small bowl. Season with salt and cracked pepper.

Dice the salmon into small pieces, place in a bowl and stir in 2½ tablespoons of the Dijon Dressing. Set aside. Store the remaining dressing in a jar in the fridge for future use.

To make the Sriracha Mayo, mix the mayonnaise and sriracha to your ideal spice level.

Gently spoon Sriracha Mayo onto the tostadas.

Evenly distribute the salmon, avocado, onion, radish and coriander between the tostadas, then garnish with the chilli and chives.

SPANISH-STYLE PRAWNS & CHORIZO WITH FOCACCIA & AIOLI

In my early 20s I lived in Palma De Mallorca, Spain, where Tapas Tuesday was a big thing. We would go out for tapas at around nine o'clock and have a few at one restaurant before moving on to the next bar in a similar fashion until the wee hours of the morning. The streets were full every Tuesday without fail. This dish reminds me of those times. I don't think I've ever consumed so much bread with aioli as I did living there.

SERVES 4

16 large raw prawns –
    defrosted
Zest of 1 lemon
1 teaspoon paprika
2 chorizo sausages
¼ cup extra virgin olive oil
3 large garlic cloves – roughly
    chopped
½ cup roughly chopped Italian
    parsley
Juice of ½ a lemon
1 red chilli – thinly sliced

TO SERVE

Fresh focaccia
Aioli

Combine the prawns, lemon zest and paprika in a bowl. Set aside.

Cut the chorizo into 1 cm (½ in) slices.

Heat a medium pan on a medium heat. Add the chorizo and fry until crispy on both sides. You don't need to add oil as the fat from the sausage will be enough. Put the cooked chorizo on a plate. Don't clean the pan.

Using the same pan, turn down the heat to medium/low. Add the olive oil and garlic and cook for 2 minutes, stirring occasionally.

Add the prawns and fry on both sides until just about cooked (this will only take a few minutes).

Return the chorizo and all its delicious oil back to the pan. Add the parsley and lemon juice and stir well.

Garnish with the chilli and serve with the focaccia and aioli.

ROASTED TOMATO & RICOTTA FLATBREAD

The way you slice this tasty flatbread will vary depending on how many people you're serving it to. If it's a little nibble then cut it into three slices each way so you can grab smaller pieces. If you're serving it as lunch for two people, cut it into six wedges. I love using seeded pizza bases, but you can use plain too.

SERVES 2–6

1 punnet cherry tomatoes
2 large garlic cloves – roughly chopped
2 tablespoons extra virgin olive oil
1 tablespoon balsamic vinegar
½ cup pesto
½ cup ricotta
1 large store-bought seeded pizza base
¾ cup zucchini ribbons
1 tablespoon pine nuts – toasted
A handful of fresh basil – roughly chopped
4 fresh thyme sprigs – tough stalks discarded
1–2 squares marinated feta – crumbled
A pinch of chilli flakes

Preheat the oven to 180°C (350°F) fan bake.

Place the tomatoes and garlic on a lined baking tray. Drizzle with the olive oil and balsamic vinegar and season with salt and cracked pepper. Roast for 25 minutes.

While the tomatoes are roasting, mix the pesto and ricotta. Smear this over the pizza base.

When the tomatoes are cooked, leave them to cool on the bench.

Turn the oven up to 220°C (425°F) fan bake. Bake the pizza base as per the packet instructions (roughly 7–10 minutes should do the trick).

When the pizza base is cooked, arrange the zucchini ribbons on top. Spoon over the tomatoes and garlic with all their delicious juices.

Top with the pine nuts, basil, thyme, crumbled feta and chilli flakes.

HEIRLOOM TOMATO & PROSCIUTTO SALAD OF YOUR DREAMS

Sometimes I create a dish and think to myself, 'WOW girlfriend, just WOW!' This is one of them. We first enjoyed this meal over a bottle of French rosé, served with a lightly toasted baguette. Although it was lockdown, the sun was shining and for a hot minute, I didn't have a care in the world.

SERVES 4 AS A STARTER

200 g (7 oz) prosciutto
2 large heirloom tomatoes –
    cut into 1 cm (½ in) rounds
12 heirloom cherry tomatoes –
    halved
2 baby cucumbers – angle-
    sliced into small chunks
1 cup roughly chopped fresh
    basil
⅓ cup roughly chopped fresh
    dill
180 g (6 oz) stracciatella
    cheese

CHILLI DRESSING

1 tablespoon chilli oil
2 tablespoons extra virgin
    olive oil
2 teaspoons red wine vinegar
2 teaspoons sugar
Juice of 1 lemon

TO SERVE

Fresh baguette – heated in the
    oven for a few minutes

To make the Chilli Dressing, whisk the ingredients in a small bowl. Set aside.

Arrange half the prosciutto on a serving platter.

Scatter most of the tomatoes and cucumber on top.

Layer on the remaining prosciutto and half the basil and dill.

Using a fork, break up the stracciatella and layer it over the top.

Add the remaining tomatoes and cucumber.

Drizzle with the dressing, scatter with the remaining basil and dill and season with salt and cracked pepper.

Serve with the warm baguette.

PUMPKIN & KUMARA SOUP WITH GREMOLATA

This is an extremely comforting soup packed full of flavour with the help of my dear friend gremolata! It's my go-to winter delivery meal when someone is in need of a pick-me-up.

SERVES 4

1 large golden kumara
3 tablespoons olive oil
1.2 kg (2 lb 10 oz) pumpkin
1 large brown onion – cut into
   8 wedges
4 large garlic cloves – roughly
   chopped
4 cups vegetable stock
1 teaspoon paprika
7 large fresh thyme sprigs –
   tough stalks discarded
¾ cup coconut milk
¼ cup pumpkin seeds –
   toasted

GREMOLATA

1 cup Italian parsley
1 cup fresh basil
⅓ cup extra virgin olive oil
1 large garlic clove
Zest and juice of 1 lemon
A pinch of chilli flakes

Preheat the oven to 200°C (400°F) fan bake.

Peel the kumara and cut into 2 cm (¾ in) chunks. Place on a lined baking tray and drizzle with the olive oil. Season with salt and cracked pepper. Roast for 25 minutes or until soft.

Cut the skin off the pumpkin and discard the seeds. Chop the flesh into large chunks. Place in a large saucepan with the onion, garlic, stock, paprika and thyme and bring to a simmer. Turn down the heat to medium and let it simmer for 15 minutes or until the pumpkin is soft.

To make the Gremolata, blitz all ingredients in a food processor until smooth. Set aside.

Once the kumara is cooked, add it to the saucepan with the cooked pumpkin. Turn off the heat.

Using a stick blender, whizz the soup until it is a smooth consistency. Carefully stir in the coconut milk.

Serve with as much Gremolata spooned on top as your heart desires and a sprinkling of pumpkin seeds.

SALADS &
SIDES

BEAUTIFUL HEIRLOOM TOMATO & STRACCIATELLA SALAD

This is an adaptation of my favourite salad from Pici restaurant in Auckland's St Kevin's Arcade. Their food is illegally good. Fresh and super easy to throw together, this is great alongside a fresh bowl of pasta, much like my Prawn & Scallop Spaghetti on page 104.

SERVES 4–5

2 tablespoons chardonnay vinegar
1 teaspoon sugar
2 tablespoons extra virgin olive oil
180 g (6 oz) stracciatella cheese
2 large heirloom tomatoes – cut into 5 mm (¼ in) slices
1 large nectarine – cut into thin wedges
2 tablespoons fresh thyme
½ cup roughly chopped fresh basil

Mix the vinegar, sugar and olive oil in a small bowl.

Spread the stracciatella over a serving platter or plates.

Arrange the tomatoes and nectarine on top of the cheese.

Sprinkle with the thyme and basil.

Drizzle the dressing over the salad and season with salt and cracked pepper.

GRILLED NECTARINE & PEACH SUMMER SALAD

The first time I made this salad I was in Hawke's Bay for Easter with friends. In spite of a nasty hangover, I volunteered to cook lunch for all 26 of us — brilliant. Luckily, this salad delivered so much flavour for how simple it was that the whole thing ended up being an absolute hoot. Since then, this dish has been one of my favourite go-tos. If you want to bulk it out more, add some fresh tomatoes and avocado chunks. Store the remaining dressing in a jar in the fridge and save for another day.

SERVES 4

1 small shallot – very thinly sliced
2 tablespoons red wine vinegar
1 teaspoon caster sugar
2 tablespoons olive oil
2 nectarines – cut into 8 wedges
2 large peaches – cut into 8 wedges
250 g (9 oz) green beans – trimmed
2 cups rocket leaves
1 cup roughly chopped fresh basil
2 fresh burrata balls
1½ tablespoons pine nuts – toasted

HONEY MUSTARD DRESSING

Juice of 1 lemon
¼ cup extra virgin olive oil
1 tablespoon wholegrain mustard
1 heaped teaspoon honey

Mix the shallot with the vinegar and sugar in a small bowl. Set aside.

To make the Honey Mustard Dressing, whisk the ingredients in a small bowl. Set aside.

Heat a griddle pan on medium/high heat. Add the olive oil. When the pan is hot, fry the nectarine and peach wedges in batches. This will take roughly 1 minute each side or until they have a bit of colour. Set aside to cool.

Using the same griddle pan, fry the beans for roughly 1½–2 minutes, stirring constantly. Set aside to cool.

Gently fold together the beans, nectarines, peaches, rocket and half the basil in a bowl.

Carefully transfer the salad to a serving platter. Discard the vinegar from the shallots, then scatter the shallots on top of the salad.

Place the burrata balls in the middle of the platter, slicing them down the middle. Drizzle 5 tablespoons of Honey Mustard Dressing over the salad. Store the remaining dressing in a jar in the fridge for future use.

Scatter the pine nuts and remaining basil on top.

EGGPLANT & CAULIFLOWER SALAD WITH CANDIED NUTS

I know what you're thinking . . . look at the size of that ingredient list. But I promise this salad is actually easy to put together. Plus, this combination of ingredients makes for a flavour explosion that you won't soon forget. Goodbye boring barbecue salads! This is basically a meal in itself.

SERVES 4–5

1 large eggplant – cut into 2 cm (¾ in) cubes
½ large head cauliflower – cut into bite-sized florets
1 tablespoon sumac
1 tablespoon cumin seeds
1 tablespoon dried oregano
⅓ cup olive oil
2 cups roughly chopped baby spinach leaves
1 cup roughly chopped Italian parsley
150 g (5½ oz) feta – roughly crumbled
½ cup chopped marinated artichoke hearts
½ cup green olives – pitted
2 tablespoons capers
1 small shallot – finely diced
2 tablespoons maple syrup
Zest of 1 large lemon
1–2 tablespoons balsamic vinegar
Juice of ½ a lemon
½ cup store-bought candied nuts
edible flowers, for garnish (optional)

Preheat the oven to 190°C (375°F) fan bake.

Place the eggplant in a single layer on a lined baking tray.

Place the cauliflower florets on a second lined baking tray.

Sprinkle the sumac, cumin seeds and oregano evenly over both trays. Drizzle both trays with the olive oil, using the majority for the eggplant. Season well with salt and cracked pepper. Roast for 35 minutes.

After 35 minutes remove the eggplant and leave the cauliflower to cook for a further 10 minutes.

While the vegetables are cooking, combine the spinach and parsley in a serving bowl. Set aside.

Mix the feta, artichokes, olives, capers, shallot, maple syrup and lemon zest in a small bowl. Set aside.

When the cauliflower and eggplant are cooked, set aside to cool for 10 minutes. When cooled, add to the serving bowl then gently fold in the feta mixture. Drizzle with the balsamic vinegar and lemon juice and scatter with the candied nuts and edible flowers (if using).

THE ULTIMATE GREEN SALAD

My girlfriends Lucinda and Sophie call this my 'absolute signature salad' and both said that if it didn't make it into the book, I had something seriously wrong with me. Well gals, here it is, just for you. Simple to make, full of flavour and destined to suit any main dish, it really is no wonder that this has become a signature of mine. Time to make it one of yours too.

SERVES 4

120 g (4¼ oz) rocket leaves
2 zucchini – cut into ribbons using a peeler
½ cup peas – defrosted
1 large spring onion – thinly sliced
½ cup roughly chopped Italian parsley
1 cup roughly chopped fresh basil
1 large avocado – flesh sliced
1 cup shaved parmesan
½ cup roasted cashews – roughly chopped
1 red chilli – thinly sliced

THE ULTIMATE VINAIGRETTE

½ cup olive oil
1 tablespoon sugar
1 tablespoon red wine vinegar
1 tablespoon Dijon mustard

To make The Ultimate Vinaigrette, whisk the ingredients in a small bowl. Season with salt and cracked pepper. Set aside.

In a large serving bowl, mix the rocket, zucchini, peas, spring onion, parsley and basil.

Gently toss in the avocado and parmesan. Top with the cashews and chilli.

Season well with salt and cracked pepper and serve with the Vinaigrette on the side.

GREEKISH SALAD

This was one of the first salad recipes I ever posted on my Instagram page, @miss_pollys_kitchen. It has a special place in my heart for the way it reminds me of the salads my mum used to make — although she used tasty cheese, not feta. Fresh and fulfilling, it can be served on its own, or you could whip up some chicken skewers or lamb rump and serve it with pita pockets on the side. Wham bam, thank you ma'am, that's one easy summer dinner!

SERVES 4

1 red capsicum – diced into small chunks
1 large avocado – flesh diced
1 punnet cherry tomatoes – halved
¾ cucumber – diced into small chunks
½ red onion – finely diced
½ cup kalamata olives – pitted and halved
1 cup roughly chopped Italian parsley
1 cup roughly chopped fresh mint
1 green chilli – finely sliced
¼ cup extra virgin olive oil
½ tablespoon red wine vinegar
Juice of ½ a lemon
150 g (5½ oz) feta – cut into chunks

Mix the capsicum, avocado, cherry tomatoes, cucumber, onion, olives, parsley, mint and chilli in a serving bowl. Set aside.

In a separate bowl, whisk the olive oil, vinegar and lemon juice. Season with salt and cracked pepper. Drizzle over the salad, then fold in the feta and serve.

THE ONE & ONLY ROASTED AUTUMN VEGETABLE SALAD

This might be the most warming and satisfying salad I've created. You could eat it on its own or with roast lamb, chicken or halloumi — and if you end up with more than you need, don't worry. Anyone who knows me knows that I seriously love leftovers, so trust me when I say it's just as tasty the next day.

SERVES 4-6

1 large golden kumara – cut into bite-sized pieces
1 large carrot – cut into bite-sized pieces
1 large parsnip – cut into bite-sized pieces
2 beetroot – cut into bite-sized pieces
1 red onion – cut into 8 wedges
1 garlic bulb – top sliced off to expose the cloves
¼ cup olive oil
1 tablespoon dried Italian herbs
100 g (3½ oz) baby kale – roughly chopped
2 oranges – peeled and segmented
1 cup roughly chopped fresh basil
100 g (3½ oz) feta – crumbled
½ cup shaved parmesan
½ cup roughly chopped Italian parsley
3 tablespoons pumpkin seeds – toasted
3 tablespoons roasted almonds
Juice of ½ a lemon
A drizzle of extra virgin olive oil

Preheat the oven to 200°C (400°F) fan bake.

Divide the kumara, carrot, parsnip, beetroot, onion and garlic between two lined baking trays, drizzle with the olive oil, sprinkle with the Italian herbs and season well with salt and cracked pepper.

Roast for 35–45 minutes, until cooked, then allow to cool for 10 minutes.

Transfer to a large serving bowl or platter. Add the kale, orange segments and half the basil and mix gently.

Top with the feta, parmesan, parsley, pumpkin seeds, almonds and the remaining basil.

Squeeze the lemon juice over the salad, then drizzle with extra virgin olive oil.

ROASTED CHERRY TOMATO SALAD

Roasted cherry tomatoes have so much flavour; they are sweet and ever so juicy. If you are making this ahead of time, keep the cooked tomatoes separate until just before serving. This is one of the easiest salads I make.

SERVES 4

1 punnet cherry tomatoes
4 garlic cloves – roughly chopped
3 tablespoons extra virgin olive oil
1 tablespoon balsamic vinegar
120 g (4¼ oz) rocket leaves
1 large avocado – flesh sliced
1 cup roughly chopped fresh basil
⅓ cup roasted almonds – roughly chopped
¾ cup shaved parmesan

Preheat the oven to 180°C (350°F) fan bake.

Place the cherry tomatoes and garlic on a lined baking tray. Drizzle with olive oil and balsamic vinegar. Season with salt and cracked pepper.

Roast for 25 minutes then allow to cool.

Gently mix the rocket, avocado, basil and almonds on a serving platter.

Once the tomatoes have cooled, carefully pour them and their beautiful juices over the salad and top with the parmesan.

GREEN QUINOA HARISSA SALAD

The flavour in this salad is punchy as hell. Simply serve it as a meal on its own or add some pan-fried salmon for a more fulfilling option.

SERVES 6

1 cup quinoa
½ head broccoli – cut into florets
1 cup frozen peas
1 zucchini – cut into ribbons using a peeler
1 cup shaved parmesan
1 cup roughly chopped Italian parsley
1 cup roughly chopped fresh basil
1 large avocado – flesh cut into chunks
Zest of 1 mandarin

CARAMELISED ALMONDS

½ cup raw almonds
1 teaspoon cumin seeds
A pinch of chilli flakes
2 tablespoons maple syrup

HARISSA VINAIGRETTE

2 tablespoons tahini
2 tablespoons olive oil
2 tablespoons lemon juice
1 tablespoon harissa paste
1 tablespoon maple syrup
1 tablespoon water

Start by cooking the quinoa as per the packet instructions. Set aside to cool.

Bring a saucepan of water to the boil on a high heat. Add the broccoli florets and boil for 1 minute, then add the peas and simmer for a further minute. Drain well.

Roughly chop the broccoli florets. Set aside.

To make the Caramelised Almonds, heat a small pan on medium heat. Add the almonds, cumin seeds and chilli flakes and cook, stirring, for roughly 4 minutes until lightly toasted. Turn off the heat. Add the maple syrup and mix it around until the almonds are coated. Tip onto a lined baking tray to cool. Once cooled, roughly chop the almonds into chunks.

To make the Harissa Vinaigrette, whisk the ingredients in a small bowl. Season with salt and cracked pepper.

Combine the cooled quinoa in a serving bowl with the broccoli, peas, zucchini ribbons, parmesan and half the parsley and basil. Fold in the avocado.

Drizzle the Harissa Vinaigrette over the salad. Sprinkle with the Caramelised Almonds and remaining parsley and basil, then zest the mandarin over the top.

PICKLED GREEN APPLE & ZUCCHINI SALAD WITH ZESTY RICOTTA

This salad is divine served with a simple tomato pasta. I particularly love the flavour you get from soaking the apples in a dressing and topping the salad with a zesty ricotta. Need I say more?

SERVES 4

2 tablespoons extra virgin olive oil
1½ tablespoons red wine vinegar
1 tablespoon Dijon mustard
1 tablespoon sugar
1 green apple – diced
½ shallot – thinly sliced
120 g (4¼ oz) rocket leaves
1 large zucchini – cut into ribbons using a peeler
1 cup roughly chopped fresh basil (plus extra leaves for garnish)
1 cup roughly chopped fresh mint (plus extra leaves for garnish)
1 avocado – flesh diced
3 tablespoons pine nuts – toasted
150 g (5½ oz) ricotta
1 tablespoon extra virgin olive oil
Zest of 1 lemon
Juice of ½ a lemon

Mix the olive oil, vinegar, mustard and sugar in a bowl, then add the apple and shallot. Season with salt and cracked pepper. Leave to marinate for 10 minutes.

Toss together the rocket, zucchini, basil and mint on a serving platter. Gently fold in the avocado and pine nuts.

In a separate bowl, mix the ricotta, olive oil, lemon zest and lemon juice. Season with cracked pepper.

Spoon the apple and its marinating juices over the salad.

Dot spoonfuls of the ricotta mixture on top of the salad and garnish with the extra basil and mint.

CRISPY POTATOES WITH ROASTED CAPSICUM

Crispy taties make a side dish that never disappoints, and the key to perfect crispiness is ensuring you drain the potatoes really, really well. Heating the oil in the tray beforehand is also essential but if you don't want delightful little oil burns all over your hands (like yours truly) please be careful!

SERVES 5 AS A SIDE

1 kg (2 lb 4 oz) medium potatoes – peeled and quartered
Extra virgin olive oil
2 large red capsicums – halved
1 garlic bulb – top sliced off to expose the cloves
A handful of Italian parsley – roughly chopped

Preheat the oven to 220°C (425°F) fan bake.

Bring a large saucepan of water to the boil on a high heat. Add the potatoes and parboil for 7 minutes.

Pour enough olive oil onto a large metal baking tray to thinly coat the base of the tray.

Once the potatoes are parboiled, drain them really well. Put the potatoes back into the saucepan with the lid on and shake a few times to roughen up the edges. Place the oiled tray into the oven to heat for 3 minutes.

Carefully take the hot oiled tray out of the oven and very gently pour the potatoes onto the tray. Turn the potatoes to coat them in the oil. Season well with salt and cracked pepper. Roast on the top shelf of the oven for 30 minutes.

When the potatoes have been cooking for 10 minutes, place the capsicums and garlic on a second tray. Drizzle with 2 tablespoons extra virgin olive oil and season with salt and cracked pepper. Working quickly to keep the heat in the oven, place the tray on the lower shelf of the oven. Roast for 20 minutes.

Place the cooked potatoes on a serving platter. Thinly slice the cooked capsicums. Add to the potatoes along with the parsley and toss to combine. Place the garlic bulb on the side of the platter so your guests can help themselves.

Serve immediately for ultimate crispiness.

BROCCOLI & CAULIFLOWER STEAKS WITH ROMESCO SAUCE

This is a seriously impressive side. I love the slightly charred taste on the veggies. That said, I would probably eat anything if it had romesco sauce drizzled over it. My advice? Make more of this sauce than you need, and next time you pan-fry some fish or barbecue a leg of lamb, pull it out of the fridge and pour generously.

SERVES 6 AS A SIDE

1 large head broccoli
1 large head cauliflower
Olive oil, for frying
A handful of Italian parsley –
    roughly chopped

ROMESCO SAUCE

465 g (1 lb) jar roasted
    capsicums – drained
⅓ cup extra virgin olive oil
⅓ cup roasted unsalted
    almonds
¼ cup Italian parsley
2 garlic cloves
1 tablespoon red wine vinegar
1 teaspoon smoked paprika
1 teaspoon sugar
Juice of ½ a lemon
A pinch of cayenne pepper

To make the Romesco Sauce, blitz all the ingredients in a food processor. Season with salt and cracked pepper. Set aside.

Slice the broccoli and cauliflower into 1 cm (½ in) steaks.

Heat a griddle pan on a high heat. Add a little olive oil. When the pan is hot, fry the broccoli and cauliflower in batches for 2–3 minutes on each side, adding a little more oil as needed. Put the lid on while cooking.

As the broccoli and cauliflower are cooked, place them on a serving platter.

Spoon the majority of the Romesco Sauce over the broccoli and cauliflower, then top with parsley. Serve with the remaining Romesco Sauce in a small ramekin on the side.

BAKED CABBAGE
WITH PARSLEY PESTO

My love of baked cabbage started when I visited a restaurant in Auckland called Candela. They serve hands-down the best baked cabbage I've ever eaten, so here is my take on it. Using parsley in the pesto makes for a nice change from the classic basil and creates a seriously saucy topping. Simple but impressive, this dish is an unexpected showstopper. She's tasty and slightly chunky (the cabbage, not me).

SERVES 4

½ white cabbage
Juice of 1 juicy lemon
A drizzle of olive oil

PARSLEY PESTO

1 cup Italian parsley
½ cup extra virgin olive oil
½ cup roasted almonds
½ cup grated parmesan
2 garlic cloves
Juice of 1 juicy lemon

TO SERVE

⅓ cup shaved parmesan

Preheat the oven to 200°C (400°F) fan bake.

Chop the cabbage into quarters and place on a lined baking tray. Drizzle with the lemon juice and olive oil. Season well with salt and cracked pepper.

Roast for 20 minutes until the cabbage is soft, with a few charred leaves.

To make the Parsley Pesto, blitz all the ingredients in a food processor until smooth. Season to taste with salt and cracked pepper.

Take the cabbage out of the oven. Spoon the Parsley Pesto evenly over the cut sides of the cabbage pieces. Put the cabbage back in the oven for 3 minutes, then garnish with the shaved parmesan and serve immediately.

ASPARAGUS WITH A TOMATO SALSA & GARLIC CRUMB

This is a light and tasty summer side dish, perfect for a family barbecue or to take to Christmas lunch. It goes exceptionally well with a piece of pan-fried fresh fish.

SERVES 4

1 slice wholegrain bread – toasted (I use Vogel's)
3 tablespoons olive oil
2 garlic cloves – very finely diced
1 small shallot – very thinly sliced
Juice of 1 lemon
2 tablespoons capers
500 g (1 lb 2 oz) asparagus – tough ends snapped off
½ punnet cherry tomatoes – quartered
½ cup finely chopped Italian parsley
2 tablespoons extra virgin olive oil
⅓ cup shaved parmesan

Put the toast in a food processor and blitz to a crumb.

Heat a small pan over a medium heat. Add 1 tablespoon of the olive oil. Add the garlic and fry for 1 minute. Next add the breadcrumbs and fry until they turn a deep gold colour. Pour them onto a plate to cool.

Place the shallot in a medium bowl. Add the lemon juice. Set aside.

Return the small pan to the heat. Fry the capers in the remaining 2 tablespoons of olive oil until crispy. Set aside to cool on paper towels.

Bring a deep pan of water to the boil on a high heat. Blanch the asparagus spears for 1–1½ minutes, depending on their thickness. Plunge them straight into a bowl of ice-cold water then drain and pat dry with paper towels.

Add the tomatoes and parsley to the shallot and lemon juice, then add the extra virgin olive oil. Season with cracked pepper and stir well. Set aside.

Place the asparagus on a serving platter, slicing any large stalks down the middle lengthways.

Scatter the parmesan over the asparagus. Spoon the tomato salsa over the top, then sprinkle with the garlic crumbs and crispy capers.

CRISPY GOLDEN KUMARA WEDGES WITH A CREAMY AVOCADO TAHINI SAUCE

Golden kumara is the sweetest member of the sweet potato family and is my personal favourite. Designed to jazz up the classic (but often boring) side of baked kumara with a hint of fiesta-worthy Mexican flavour, this recipe is a great addition to any roast dinner or barbecue.

SERVES 4

2 large golden kumara
2 tablespoons olive oil
1 tablespoon smoked paprika
⅓ cup pumpkin seeds – toasted
⅓ cup finely chopped jalapeños
A small handful of fresh coriander – roughly chopped

CREAMY AVOCADO TAHINI SAUCE

Flesh of 1 large avocado
1 cup fresh coriander
1 cup fresh basil
½ cup thick Greek yoghurt
2 tablespoons extra virgin olive oil
1½ tablespoons tahini
Juice of 1 lemon

Preheat the oven to 190°C (375°F) fan bake.

Chop the kumara into wedges, leaving the skin on. Place on a lined baking tray. Drizzle with the olive oil, sprinkle with the smoked paprika and season generously with salt and cracked pepper.

Roast for 40 minutes or until cooked and slightly crispy.

To make the Creamy Avocado Tahini Sauce, blitz all the ingredients in a food processor until smooth.

Smear half the sauce onto the base of a serving platter and transfer the remaining sauce to a serving ramekin.

Place the cooked kumara on top of the sauce on the platter. Scatter with pumpkin seeds, jalapeños and coriander and serve with the extra sauce on the side.

CAPONATA

I learned how to make this when I stayed at Masseria Potenti in Puglia, which is one of the most incredible places to visit. (The chef there, Alessandro, is equally divine, by the way.) My friends Lucinda and Mikayla and I took a cooking class that covered focaccia and orecchiette as well. Oh the memories! This can be served hot or at room temperature, and it is the perfect side for a long lunch.

SERVES 6

2 large eggplants – cut into 2 cm (¾ in) dice
¼ cup olive oil
3 tablespoons extra virgin olive oil
1 red onion – halved and thinly sliced
4 garlic cloves – diced
2 teaspoons dried oregano
2 zucchini – diced into small pieces
1 capsicum – diced into small pieces
½ cup olives – pitted
⅓ cup raisins
⅓ cup pine nuts
2 tablespoons capers – roughly chopped
1½ tablespoons red wine vinegar
1 teaspoon soft brown sugar
400 g (14 oz) can cherry tomatoes
1 cup roughly chopped Italian parsley

Preheat the oven to 190°C (375°F) fan bake.

Place the eggplant on a lined baking tray. Drizzle with the ¼ cup of olive oil. Season with salt and cracked pepper. Bake for 25 minutes until soft.

Heat 2 tablespoons of the extra virgin olive oil in a large saucepan on a medium heat. Add the onion and a good pinch of salt. Cook for 5 minutes, stirring occasionally.

Add the garlic, oregano and the remaining tablespoon of extra virgin olive oil and cook, stirring often, for a couple more minutes.

Stir in the zucchini, capsicum, olives, raisins, pine nuts, capers, vinegar and sugar. Add the cherry tomatoes, then fill the can nearly quarter full with water, swirl it around and pour it into the saucepan.

By this point, the eggplant should be cooked. Add it to the saucepan with the vegetables, fold everything together then simmer on a low heat for 20 minutes. Stir in most of the parsley, reserving some for garnish.

Transfer the caponata to a serving platter and garnish with the remaining parsley.

VEGETARIAN

MIDDLE EASTERN-INSPIRED EGGPLANT & BUTTER BEAN TAGINE

As vegetarian meals go, this is a crowd-pleaser. It's such a warming dish for winter but also light enough to enjoy on a hot day with a crisp wine. My dad introduced me to lots of herbs and spices from a young age. That, and eating lots of eggplant (or aubergine as he called it). If he were still here, I know he would absolutely love this dish.

SERVES 5–6

6 tablespoons olive oil
3 eggplants – cut into large bite-sized pieces
1 large red onion – cut into thin wedges
1 tablespoon minced fresh ginger
4 large garlic cloves – roughly chopped
1 tablespoon ras el hanout
1 teaspoon paprika
1 teaspoon ground cumin
½ teaspoon cinnamon
Zest of 1 lemon
Juice of ½ a lemon
2 red capsicums – cut into bite-sized pieces
¼ cup tomato paste
2 x 400 g (14 oz) cans cherry tomatoes
400 g (14 oz) can butter beans – drained and rinsed
1 cup vegetable stock
1–2 teaspoons soft brown sugar
1½ cups couscous
1 cup Italian parsley – roughly chopped
A little crumbled feta
A scatter of pomegranate seeds

Heat a large wok on a medium/high heat.

Add 3 tablespoons of the olive oil. Fry the eggplant for 8–10 minutes, stirring occasionally (if you don't have a large wok you will need to do this in two batches). You want it slightly crispy but soft in the middle. Set aside in a bowl.

Heat a large saucepan on a low heat. Add 2 tablespoons of the olive oil, then the onion and ginger. Cook gently for 5 minutes until soft, being careful not to burn them.

Add the garlic, spices, lemon zest and lemon juice. Cook gently for a couple more minutes, stirring occasionally.

Add the eggplant back into the wok, then the capsicums, tomato paste and the remaining tablespoon of olive oil. Cook for a few minutes, stirring until well combined.

Add the cherry tomatoes, beans, stock and sugar. Season well with salt and cracked pepper. Mix everything together. Turn the heat to low, put the lid on and let it bubble away for 50–60 minutes.

When the tagine is nearly ready, start cooking the couscous as per the packet instructions.

When the tagine is ready, remove the lid. Add half the parsley then give it a good stir. Garnish with the feta, pomegranate seeds and the remaining parsley, and serve with the couscous.

MUSHROOM & RICOTTA PASTA

This pasta is an absolute delight, creamy but not too heavy, with the cherry tomatoes adding just the right amount of acidity. I prefer to cut the mushrooms rather chunky, so they have a good bite to them.

SERVES 4

200 g (7 oz) large portobello
  mushrooms
300 g (10½ oz) button
  mushrooms – halved
¾ cup extra virgin olive oil
350 g (12 oz) dried spaghetti
1 large shallot – thinly sliced
6 large garlic cloves – diced
⅓ cup fresh thyme sprigs –
  tough stalks discarded
½ teaspoon chilli flakes
Zest of 1 lemon
⅓ cup white wine
1 tablespoon balsamic vinegar
1 cup roughly chopped Italian
  parsley
1 cup ricotta
½ punnet cherry tomatoes –
  quartered
Juice of ½ a lemon

Bring a large saucepan of salted water to the boil on a high heat.

Cut each portobello mushroom into 4 slices and place on a plate with the halved button mushrooms. Place a large pan on a medium/high heat. Add ¼ cup of the extra virgin olive oil. Add half the mushrooms and fry until they are nicely browned on both sides. Season well with salt and cracked pepper. Set aside on a plate. Cook the remaining mushrooms with another ¼ cup of oil. Once these are done, pour them onto the plate with the other cooked mushrooms.

Add the spaghetti to the boiling water and cook as per the packet instructions.

While the pasta is cooking, add the remaining ¼ cup of oil and the shallot to the pan you fried the mushrooms in. Add a pinch of salt and fry on a low heat for 3 minutes.

Add the garlic, thyme, chilli and lemon zest. Cook for a further 5 minutes, stirring occasionally.

Add the mushrooms back to the pan. Mix everything together, then turn up the heat. Add the wine, balsamic vinegar and half the parsley. Simmer for 5 minutes, stirring often. Turn off the heat and fold in the ricotta.

Drain the pasta, reserving 1 cup of pasta water.

Add the pasta to the sauce, slowly adding the pasta water as required. Toss everything together so the spaghetti is well coated. Top with the cherry tomatoes, lemon juice and the remaining parsley.

STUFFED BAKED EGGPLANT

This is a cheesy, zesty delight that goes perfectly with The Ultimate Green Salad on page 50. Use a sharp knife to score the eggplant flesh, starting at the top and going across on the diagonal both ways to create a criss-crossing pattern down to the base. It's easy to double the recipe if you're serving a bigger group.

SERVES 4 AS A LIGHT MEAL

3 large eggplants – halved
3 tablespoons olive oil
250 g (9 oz) spinach leaves
150 g (5½ oz) feta – crumbled
1 punnet cherry tomatoes – diced into eighths
½ cup sun-dried tomatoes – finely diced
½ cup ricotta
⅓ cup pesto
3 tablespoons pine nuts – toasted
1 cup roughly chopped fresh basil
2 tablespoons fresh thyme
1 tablespoon dried oregano
Zest of 1 lemon

TO SERVE

A handful of pomegranate seeds

Preheat the oven to 200°C (400°F) fan bake.

Score the flesh of the eggplants and place skin-side down on a lined baking tray. Drizzle with the olive oil. Bake for 30 minutes or until soft.

Boil a jug of water. Put the spinach in a bowl, cover with boiling water and let sit for 1 minute. Carefully pour into a colander, then run under cold water until the spinach cools. Using your hands, pick up the wilted spinach and squeeze out all the excess liquid. You will need to squeeze it a few times. Roughly chop the spinach, then pull it apart so it is no longer in a big clump.

Place the spinach in a large bowl, add the remaining ingredients and mix everything together.

When the eggplant is cooked, gently spoon the mixture evenly over the top. Season with salt and cracked pepper and bake for a further 20 minutes.

Serve with a sprinkling of pomegranate seeds.

CRISPY TOFU SOBA NOODLE SALAD

A beautiful summery meal that won't take long to throw together. I love the Asian flavours in the dressing, combined with the sweetness of the mandarin juice. Dusting the tofu in cornflour gives it a little crunch and subtle flavour. I would also make this dish with prawns or chicken. If you aren't cooking for vegetarians, you can use fish sauce instead of the coconut aminos.

SERVES 4

650 g (1 lb 7 oz) firm tofu
⅓ cup cornflour
1 tablespoon onion powder
1 tablespoon garlic powder
2 large heads bok choy
320 g (11¼ oz) soba noodles
A drizzle of oil
1 cup peas
1 avocado – flesh sliced
1 cup roughly chopped fresh
 coriander
1 cup roughly chopped fresh
 mint
¼ cup roughly chopped
 pickled ginger
1 red chilli – thinly sliced

TANGY MANDARIN DRESSING

1 medium shallot – very thinly
 sliced
2 tablespoons coconut aminos
 or fish sauce
2 tablespoons soy sauce
1 tablespoon honey
1 tablespoon sesame oil
Zest of 2 mandarins
Juice of 4 mandarins
Juice of 2 juicy limes

To make the Tangy Mandarin Dressing, whisk the ingredients in a small bowl. Set aside.

Bring a saucepan of water to the boil on a high heat.

Pat the tofu dry with paper towels. Cut the tofu into 2 cm (¾ in) slices, then cut each slice in half lengthways. Mix the cornflour, onion powder and garlic powder on a plate. Dip each piece of tofu into the cornflour mix (you want a generous coating). Set aside.

Trim off the base of the bok choy and cut the leaves crossways into 2 cm (¾ in) slices.

Add the soba noodles to the boiling water and cook as per the packet instructions. While the noodles are cooking, heat a large pan on a medium/high heat. Add enough oil to coat the bottom of the pan. Fry the tofu in batches until crispy on both sides. Set aside.

When the noodles have 30 seconds of cook time to go, add the bok choy and peas. Pour the noodles and veggies into a colander then run under cold water for roughly 20 seconds. Drain well and transfer to a serving platter.

Add the avocado and half the coriander and mint and toss gently. Arrange the tofu pieces on top of the noodles. Spoon over the chunky bits from the Tangy Mandarin Dressing, then pour over the dressing. Garnish with the ginger, chilli and the remaining coriander and mint.

CRISPY TOFU LAKSA

I know some of you must be thinking 'What in the Lord's name is she doing with Cajun spice and laksa in the same meal?' Trust me, it works a bloody treat. Oh and the best laksa paste I have found for this is Asian Home Gourmet sachets.

SERVES 4

650 g (1 lb 7 oz) firm tofu
Oil, for frying
1 brown onion – thinly sliced
3 garlic cloves – minced
1 thumb-sized piece fresh
    ginger – minced
120 g (4¼ oz) laksa paste
2 x 400 ml (14 fl oz) cans
    coconut milk
2 cups vegetable stock
250 g (9 oz) portobello
    mushrooms – cut into four
    slices
½ cup cornflour
¼ cup Cajun spice
2 eggs
1 cup panko crumbs
300 g (10½ oz) udon noodles
2 heads bok choy
1 tablespoon coconut aminos
    (or fish sauce if you're not
    vegetarian)
Juice of 1 lime
1 spring onion – thinly sliced
1 red chilli – thinly sliced
A handful of fresh coriander –
    roughly chopped
Chilli oil for serving (optional)

Preheat the oven to 120°C (235°F) fan bake.

Wrap the block of tofu in paper towels. Place something heavy on top (I use cooking books or a chopping board) and set aside for 20 minutes. Pressing out the liquid will make the tofu super crispy.

Heat a large wok on a medium heat. Add 2 tablespoons of oil and fry the onion, garlic and ginger for 5 minutes until soft. Add the laksa paste and stir for a further minute. Add the coconut milk, stock and mushrooms. Leave this to simmer away on a low heat.

Cut the tofu into 2 cm (¾ in) slices, then cut each slice in half lengthways.

Mix the cornflour with 2 tablespoons of the Cajun spice in a bowl. Whisk the eggs in a separate bowl. Mix the remaining Cajun spice with the panko crumbs on a plate. Dip the tofu pieces into the cornflour mixture, coating well. Then dip them into the egg wash and then finally into the panko mixture, pressing down firmly on each piece so they are nicely coated. Set aside on a plate.

Bring a large saucepan of water to the boil on a medium heat.

Heat a large pan on a medium/high heat. Add enough oil to coat the bottom of the pan. Fry the tofu in batches until crispy on both sides. Place in the oven to keep warm.

Cook the noodles in the boiling water, as per the packet instructions.

Continued overleaf

Trim off the base of the bok choy and cut the leaves in half lengthways. Add the bok choy to the laksa sauce and cook for 2 minutes. Add the coconut aminos or fish sauce and lime juice.

Drain the noodles and divide them between four individual bowls. Pour over the laksa, then top with the crispy tofu. Garnish with the spring onion, chilli and coriander. Serve with the chilli oil (if using).

MEXICAN KUMARA STEAKS WITH BEANS & SPICY TAHINI SAUCE

This is basically a Mexican-inspired flavour bomb in your mouth. I love having the leftovers the next day, heated up with a couple of fried eggs on top.

SERVES 4 AS A MAIN

2 large golden kumara
1–2 tablespoons olive oil
Zest of 1 lime
1 red chilli – thinly sliced

SPICY TAHINI SAUCE

2 tablespoons sriracha
2 tablespoons maple syrup
1½ tablespoons tahini
1 teaspoon paprika
½ teaspoon dried ginger
¼ teaspoon garlic powder
Juice of 1 lemon

TOMATO & AVOCADO SALSA

1 punnet cherry tomatoes
1 large avocado – flesh diced
½ cup chopped fresh coriander
Juice of ½ a lemon

BEAUTIFUL BEAN MIX

3 tablespoons olive oil
1 large red onion – diced
4 garlic cloves – diced
2 tablespoons minced ginger
1 tablespoon ground cumin
400 g (14 oz) can black
    beans – drained and rinsed
400 g (14 oz) can kidney
    beans – drained and rinsed
1 red capsicum – diced
Juice of 1 lemon
3 tablespoons soy sauce
¼ cup chopped fresh coriander

Preheat the oven to 200°C (400°F) fan bake.

Cut the kumara lengthways into 2 cm (¾ in) steaks. Place on a couple of lined baking trays, drizzle with the olive oil and sprinkle with the lime zest. Season with salt and cracked pepper. Roast for 30–40 minutes or until cooked.

While the kumara is cooking, make the Spicy Tahini Sauce by mixing the ingredients in a bowl. If you prefer a thinner consistency add a little splash of water. Set aside.

To make the Tomato & Avocado Salsa, quarter the cherry tomatoes, then mix with the remaining ingredients in a small bowl. Season well with salt and cracked pepper. Set aside.

To make the Beautiful Bean Mix, heat a large pan on a low heat. Add 2 tablespoons of the olive oil, the onion and a pinch of salt. Cook for 5 minutes until soft.

Stir in the garlic, ginger, cumin and the remaining tablespoon of olive oil. Cook gently for 3 minutes, stirring occasionally so nothing sticks.

Next, add the black beans, kidney beans, capsicum and lemon juice. Cook for 5 minutes. Mix in the soy sauce and coriander. Turn off the heat and cover with a lid.

By this point, the kumara should be done. Place the kumara steaks on a large serving platter and spoon the Beautiful Bean Mix on top. Drizzle with the Spicy Tahini Sauce and top with the Tomato and Avocado Salsa. Garnish with the chilli.

SPICED EGGPLANT & HALLOUMI PILAF

For some reason I was never big on halloumi — I avoided it for years, until one day my neighbour Caitlin made a halloumi rice dish for dinner. I was instantly converted and realised I had been missing out. Be sure to consume this straight away while the cheese is hot and crunchy!

SERVES 4

2 large eggplants – halved
About ½ cup olive oil
2 teaspoons mixed spice
1 teaspoon cumin seeds
1 large red onion – cut into
    1 cm (½ in) dice
2½ teaspoons ras el hanout
1½ cups basmati rice
4 garlic cloves – roughly
    chopped
3 cups vegetable stock
1 cinnamon stick
400 g (14 oz) halloumi
2 large firm tomatoes – cut
    into 1 cm (½ in) slices
50 g (1¾ oz) butter
½ cup pine nuts – toasted
⅓ cup pomegranate seeds
¼ cup pumpkin seeds –
    toasted
½ cup roughly chopped Italian
    parsley
½ cup roughly chopped fresh
    mint
Juice of ½ an orange

Preheat the oven to 180°C (350°F) fan bake.

Score the flesh of the eggplants. Season with salt and allow them to sit for a few minutes, then pat the flesh dry with a paper towel.

Place the eggplant halves skin-side down on a lined baking tray. Drizzle each half with 1 tablespoon of the olive oil and sprinkle evenly with the mixed spice and cumin seeds. Bake for 30 minutes or until soft. Set aside.

While the eggplant is cooking, place a large saucepan on a medium/low heat. Add 1 tablespoon of the olive oil, the onion, 1½ teaspoons of the ras el hanout and a pinch of salt. Fry for 5 minutes until soft, stirring occasionally.

Add the rice and garlic. Stir for a minute so the rice is well coated. Add the stock and cinnamon stick. Gently stir.

Put the lid on and turn the heat to low. Let it bubble away for 15–20 minutes until cooked.

Cut the halloumi into 1 cm (½ in) slices. Pat it dry, then sprinkle the remaining 1 teaspoon of ras el hanout over both sides.

Heat 1 tablespoon of the olive oil in a medium pan on a medium/high heat. Sprinkle the tomato slices with salt and cracked pepper and fry them for 1 minute per side. Transfer to a large serving dish.

Continued overleaf

By this point, the rice should be done. Add the butter to the rice, let it sit for 5 minutes with the lid on, then stir it through.

Cut the cooked eggplant into large chunks and add this to the serving dish.

Add a good splash of olive oil to a non-stick pan on a medium heat. When the pan is hot, fry the halloumi until crispy on both sides.

While the halloumi is cooking, add the rice to the serving dish. Remove and discard the cinnamon stick and mix the rice through the eggplant and tomatoes. Add the pine nuts, pomegranate seeds and pumpkin seeds, then add the parsley and mint, reserving a handful for the garnish.

Top with the cooked halloumi and the remaining parsley and mint. Squeeze the orange juice over the top and serve.

BAKED LEMON RISOTTO

I know, I know, this is anything but traditional, but sometimes you need a little cheat-meal and this is one of them. If you like fish, a pan-fried piece of snapper goes very well with this! If you're vegetarian, grill some 1 cm (½ in) zucchini slices to serve on the side, or roast some balsamic cherry tomatoes as in the recipe on page 36.

SERVES 4

50 g (1¾ oz) butter
2 brown onions – diced
7 large garlic cloves – finely diced
Zest of 2 lemons
2 cups arborio rice
¾ cup white wine
4½ cups hot vegetable stock
150 g (5½ oz) parmesan – grated
1 cup finely chopped Italian parsley
Juice of ½ a lemon
⅓ cup finely chopped fresh chives
⅓ cup roughly chopped fresh dill
A good pinch of chilli flakes

Preheat the oven to 200°C (400°F) fan bake.

Melt the butter in a large, deep ovenproof pan on a medium/low heat. Add the onion and a good pinch of salt and cook until the onion is nice and soft, stirring occasionally to prevent burning. Add the garlic and continue to cook for roughly 3 minutes until soft. Mix through the zest of 1 lemon.

Add the rice, then pour in the wine. Simmer, stirring constantly, until the wine is absorbed.

Add 4 cups of the hot stock. Season with salt and cracked pepper. Stir well, then cover with a lid or 2 layers of tin foil. Carefully place the dish in the oven and bake for 24–28 minutes until cooked.

When the risotto is cooked, stir in the parmesan, parsley, lemon juice and the remaining ½ cup of stock.

Top with the chives, dill, chilli flakes and the remaining lemon zest. Serve immediately.

GREEN VEGGIE FRIED RICE

Fried rice is always best using leftover rice. However, if you don't have any handy, just cook your rice as normal and let it cool for a bit on a plate. I like to add a splash more soy sauce and a squeeze of lemon juice to my serving. And of course some chilli oil, darling.

SERVES 4–6

3 tablespoons light cooking oil
1 large brown onion – diced
5 garlic cloves – finely diced
1 cup peas
1 cup angle-sliced bok choy
1½ cups diced zucchini
1½ teaspoons sesame oil
3 large eggs
4 cups cold cooked rice
¼ teaspoon white pepper
2 tablespoons mirin
2 tablespoons oyster sauce
2 tablespoons soy sauce
½ cup roasted cashews –
    roughly chopped
1 spring onion – thinly sliced

TO SERVE
Chilli oil

Heat 2 tablespoons of the cooking oil in a large wok over a medium/low heat. Add the onion and a good pinch of salt. Cook for 5 minutes until soft, stirring occasionally.

Add the garlic and cook for a further 3 minutes, adding a splash more oil if required.

Add the peas, bok choy and zucchini and cook for 4 minutes, stirring occasionally.

Move the veggies to the side of the wok. Add the remaining tablespoon of cooking oil and ½ teaspoon of the sesame oil.

Crack the eggs into the wok. Working quickly, use a cooking spatula to scramble the eggs until cooked.

Mix the vegetables and eggs. Add the cold rice and gently fold everything together.

Add the white pepper, mirin, oyster sauce, soy sauce and the remaining 1 teaspoon sesame oil and keep folding everything together until the rice has heated through. Garnish with the cashews and spring onion.

SEAFOOD

GINGER HAPUKA STIR-FRY

Everyone needs a good stir-fry recipe and this one has never let me down. It's quick and simple to make and, in my experience, always a total crowd-pleaser. Hot tip: always, always start this dish by slicing and dicing your ingredients and prepping your sauces. This will make everything else feel seamless and stress-free.

SERVES 3

¾ cup white rice
550 g (1 lb 4 oz) boneless, skinless hapuka
¼ cup cornflour
½ teaspoon white pepper
5½ tablespoons light cooking oil
1 large eggplant – cut into 2 cm (¾ in) dice
4 cm (1½ inch) piece fresh ginger – finely diced
3 large garlic cloves – finely diced
Green part of 1 spring onion – thinly sliced
1 red chilli – thinly sliced
A handful of fresh coriander – roughly chopped

STIR-FRY SAUCE

¼ cup soy sauce
2 tablespoons sweet chilli sauce
1 teaspoon sesame oil

Get the rice cooking as per the packet instructions.

To make the Stir-Fry Sauce, mix the ingredients in a small bowl. Set aside.

Cut the fish into 2 cm (¾ in) pieces. Mix the cornflour and white pepper on a plate. Coat the fish pieces with the cornflour. Set aside.

Heat 2½ tablespoons of the oil in a large non-stick pan over a high heat. Add the eggplant and ginger and cook for 5 minutes, stirring often so the eggplant cooks evenly. It should be slightly coloured but not burned, so adjust the heat accordingly.

Add a further 1 tablespoon of oil and the garlic to the pan. Stir, then continue to fry for about 3 minutes, or until the eggplant is cooked. Be sure to keep an eye on it and keep stirring. Once the eggplant is cooked, tip it onto a plate and set aside.

Using the same pan, keep the heat on high. Add the remaining 2 tablespoons of oil. Once you see light wisps of smoke, fry the fish pieces until they are crispy on both sides. This will only take a couple of minutes. Be careful not to overcook the fish.

Return the eggplant to the pan, add the Stir-Fry Sauce and simmer for 20 seconds. Quickly take the pan off the heat.

Garnish with the spring onion, chilli and coriander. Serve immediately with the rice.

SMOKED FISH CAKES

Fish cakes are always a winner in my household. While they definitely satisfy most weeknight cravings, they're also spectacular when served on a sunny day alongside a crisp glass of white wine. These are a great hosting hack if you're entertaining and need to whip up some canapés — simply reduce the patty size by rolling the batter into smaller balls.

SERVES 4–5

450 g (1 lb) medium potatoes
200 g (7 oz) boneless, skinless smoked white fish
200 g (7 oz) boneless, skinless white fish fillets
½ cup mayonnaise (I use Kewpie)
2 tablespoons capers
1 tablespoon Dijon mustard
Zest of 1 lemon
2 spring onions – thinly sliced
½ cup finely chopped Italian parsley
½ cup finely chopped fresh dill
½ cup panko crumbs
1 egg
¼ cup light cooking oil
Lemon or lime wedges, for squeezing

HERBY MAYONNAISE

½ cup mayonnaise (I use Best Foods)
¼ cup lemon juice
A handful of fresh dill – finely chopped
½ teaspoon paprika

Bring a large saucepan of water to the boil on a high heat. Peel and quarter the potatoes, add to the pot and simmer for 10 minutes or until soft.

While the potatoes are cooking, blitz the smoked fish, fresh fish, mayonnaise, capers, mustard and lemon zest in a food processor until smooth.

Drain the potatoes well. Place them into a large mixing bowl and mash until smooth. Add the fish mixture, spring onions, parsley, dill, panko crumbs and egg. Season with salt and cracked pepper. Mix until well combined.

Using your hands, roll the mixture into 8 balls. Press down on top of each ball to create a flat patty.

Heat two large non-stick pans on a medium/low heat. Add 2 tablespoons of oil to each pan. Fry the fish cakes for 5 minutes on each side.

While the fish cakes are cooking, mix the Herby Mayonnaise ingredients in a small serving bowl. Season with salt and cracked pepper. Set aside.

Serve the fish cakes on a large serving platter with the Herby Mayonnaise and lemon or lime wedges on the side.

PRAWN & SCALLOP SPAGHETTI

Two words. SERIOUSLY. DELICIOUS. If you are a seafood lover like me, this pasta should be top of your list to make this summer! Perfectly al dente and slightly spicy, this dish packs an oh-so-flavoursome punch without requiring too much fuss at all, and is perfect for a long late-afternoon lunch. Be aware: you might not need to use all the pasta water, so add it slowly.

SERVES 4

½ cup extra virgin olive oil
10 garlic cloves – very thinly sliced
⅓ cup white wine
1 teaspoon chilli flakes
Zest of 2 lemons
1 cup roughly chopped Italian parsley
400 g (14 oz) dried or fresh spaghetti
400 g (14 oz) raw prawns – defrosted
300 g (10½ oz) raw scallops
½ cup grated parmesan
1 punnet cherry tomatoes – halved
150 g (5½ oz) feta – broken into small chunks
1 cup roughly chopped fresh basil

Bring a large saucepan of salted water to the boil on a high heat.

Heat a large pan on a low heat. Add the olive oil and garlic and cook for a few minutes, stirring occasionally. Stir in the wine, chilli, lemon zest and half the parsley. Simmer for 4–5 minutes until the alcohol burns off, then turn off the heat.

Get the spaghetti cooking in the boiling water as per the packet instructions.

When the pasta has 3 minutes of cooking time to go, reheat the garlic sauce over a medium/low heat. Add the prawns and scallops. Season with salt and cracked pepper. Cook for a few minutes, turning halfway, until just cooked through.

Drain the pasta, reserving 1 cup of pasta water.

Add the cooked pasta to the sauce. Stir in the parmesan and the remaining parsley. Add as much reserved pasta water as required to loosen everything up.

Stir through the cherry tomatoes and sprinkle with chunks of feta. Garnish with the basil.

DUKKAH-BAKED SALMON WITH A HERBY SALSA

This goes beautifully with a fresh loaf of bread or the Grilled Nectarine & Peach Summer Salad on page 46. I also love to serve it with artisan crackers and a ramekin of aioli, as something tasty to nibble on when friends come around. You can make it ahead of time and serve it cold.

SERVES 4–5 AS A MAIN

3 tablespoons dukkah
2 tablespoons lime juice
1 heaped tablespoon honey
1 teaspoon cumin seeds
2 garlic cloves – minced
1 kg (2 lb 4 oz) side boneless,
　skinless salmon

HERBY SALSA

Juice of 1 juicy lime
1 teaspoon sugar
2 tablespoons pickled
　jalapeños – finely diced
½ cup finely chopped Italian
　parsley
½ cup finely chopped fresh dill
¼ cup finely chopped fresh
　chives

Preheat the oven to 200°C (400°F) fan bake.

Mix the dukkah, lime juice, honey, cumin seeds and garlic in a small bowl.

Place the salmon skin-side down on a lined baking tray. Spoon the dukkah mixture over the salmon. Season with salt and cracked pepper.

Bake for roughly 16 minutes (the cook time will vary depending on the thickness of the salmon).

While the salmon is cooking, make the Herby Salsa. Whisk the lime juice and sugar in a bowl, then add the jalapeños, parsley, dill and chives. Season with salt and cracked pepper. Set aside.

Once the salmon is cooked, gently lift it onto a serving platter and spoon the salsa over the top.

CRISPY-SKINNED FISH WITH SALSA & BABY CARROTS

As the summer nights get longer and warmer, pan-fried fish becomes one of my favourite meals. I've found the key to perfect fish is to keep it simple and fresh. Adding a salsa delivers so much flavour. One important thing to note with fish is that it will keep cooking when you take it off the heat, so be careful not to overcook it.

SERVES 4

500 g (1 lb 2 oz) baby carrots – trimmed
2 tablespoons fresh thyme
1 tablespoon fennel seeds
2 tablespoons honey
¼ cup extra virgin olive oil
150 g (5½ oz) feta – broken into chunks
4 large skin-on, boneless white fish fillets
2 tablespoons butter

HERBALICIOUS SALSA

½ cup extra virgin olive oil
3 tablespoons lemon juice
⅓ cup roasted almonds – finely chopped
3 tablespoons capers – finely chopped
1 cup finely chopped Italian parsley
½ cup finely chopped fresh basil

Preheat the oven to 180°C (350°F) fan bake.

Place the carrots, thyme and fennel seeds on a lined baking tray. Drizzle with the honey and 2 tablespoons of the olive oil. Season with salt and cracked pepper. Roast for 15 minutes.

Remove the tray from the oven. Turn the carrots. Scatter the feta over the top. Place back in the oven for a further 10–15 minutes.

While the carrots are cooking, make the Herbalicious Salsa. Whisk the oil and lemon juice in a bowl, then add the other ingredients. Season with salt and cracked pepper and mix well. Set aside.

Pat the fish dry with paper towels and season the skin side with salt and cracked pepper.

When the carrots have roughly 5 minutes of roasting time left, heat two large non-stick pans on a medium/high heat. Add 1 tablespoon butter and 1 tablespoon of the olive oil per pan. When the pans are hot, add the fish fillets skin-side down.

Place the cooked carrots on a large serving platter.

When the flesh of the fish is mostly opaque, season it with salt and cracked pepper then flip it and cook for a further 20 seconds. Plate the fish skin-side up on four plates and spoon the Herbalicious Salsa on top. Enjoy with the side of roasted carrots.

LIME & COCONUT CRUMBED FISH BITES

Adding lime leaves to the panko crumbs takes this recipe from ordinary to legendary. Just make sure you dice them very finely. Serve this sensational take on the classic fish and chips with the Roasted Cherry Tomato Salad on page 56.

SERVES 4

3 large potatoes – washed
A drizzle of olive oil
½ cup cornflour
2 eggs
2 cups panko crumbs
¼ cup desiccated coconut
3 makrut lime leaves – very finely diced
½ cup finely chopped fresh coriander
4 x 200 g (7 oz) boneless, skinless white fish fillets
Oil, for frying

LIME MAYO

1 cup mayonnaise (I use Kewpie)
¼ cup sriracha
Juice of 1 lime

Preheat the oven to 200°C (400°F) fan bake.

Bring a large saucepan of water to the boil on a high heat. Cut the potatoes into roughly 1 cm (½ in) wedges. Parboil for 5 minutes. Drain well.

Space the wedges out on a lined baking tray. Season with salt and cracked pepper. Drizzle with a generous amount of olive oil. Roast for 30 minutes or until crispy.

While the wedges are cooking, put the cornflour on a plate. Season with salt and cracked pepper. Whisk the eggs in a bowl. Combine the panko crumbs, coconut, lime leaves and coriander on a plate.

Cut each fish fillet into three pieces. Coat each piece in cornflour, then dip it into the egg wash, then press it firmly into the panko mix, coating well. Set aside.

To make the Lime Mayo, mix the ingredients in a serving bowl. Set aside.

When the wedges have roughly 5 minutes left to cook, heat two pans on a medium heat. Pour enough oil to coat the bottom of the pan. When the pans are hot, fry the fish until golden on both sides and cooked through.

Serve alongside the potato wedges and Lime Mayo.

SPICY JALAPEÑO PRAWN TACOS

This is my all-time favourite taco recipe. If spice isn't your thing, simply omit the jalapeños from each part of the recipe, and if you want to switch things up, use fish instead of prawns. But my advice? If these tacos are on the menu, pour yourself an ice-cold passionfruit margarita and get some Buena Vista Social Club playing in the background. You can't go wrong.

SERVES 4

½ cup chopped fresh coriander
¼ cup diced pickled jalapeños
2 tablespoons Cajun spice
2 large garlic cloves – minced
Zest of 1 lime
800 g (1 lb 12 oz) raw prawns – defrosted
16 baby cos lettuce leaves
A drizzle of olive oil
Juice of 1 lime
8–10 mini soft tortillas

MANGO AVOCADO SALSA

2 avocados – flesh diced
1 large mango – flesh diced
½ red onion – finely diced
½ red chilli – finely diced
½ cup roughly chopped fresh coriander
Zest and juice of 1 lime

SPICY GREEN MAYO

⅓ cup mayonnaise
¼ cup thick Greek yoghurt
3 tablespoons pickled jalapeños
1 garlic clove
1 cup fresh coriander
½ cup fresh parsley
1 spring onion
Juice of ½ a lime

Mix the coriander, jalapeños, Cajun spice, garlic and lime zest in a large bowl. Add the prawns and stir well. Set aside.

To make the Mango Avocado Salsa, mix the ingredients in a serving bowl. Season with salt and cracked pepper. Set aside.

To make the Spicy Green Mayo, blitz the ingredients in a food processor until smooth. Pour into a serving ramekin.

Place the lettuce on a small serving plate. Set aside.

Heat two large pans over a high heat. Add enough oil to lightly coat the bottom of the pans. Once hot, divide the prawns between the pans, squeeze over the lime juice and season with salt and cracked pepper. Cook, stirring, until slightly crispy and cooked through. This will only take a few minutes.

While the prawns are frying, lightly toast the tortillas over a gas flame or in a dry pan. Once they are toasted, fold them in half and set aside on a serving plate with a tea towel draped over them to stay warm.

Place the cooked prawns in a serving bowl. Serve immediately with the salsa, mayo and tortillas on the side so everyone can help themselves.

INDIAN-INSPIRED TREVALLY & EGGPLANT CURRY

Not only easy to whip up, this Indian-inspired curry is also seriously flavoursome. It's important to note that when you turn off the element, the heat from the sauce will continue to cook the fish, so keep a close eye on the timing and take the pan off the heat just before the fish is completely cooked through.

SERVES 4

1½ cups basmati rice
About ¼ cup light olive oil
1 large brown onion – diced
1 large eggplant – cut into
    2 cm (¾ in) chunks
5 large garlic cloves – roughly
    chopped
2 tablespoons minced fresh
    ginger
1 tablespoon garam masala
1 teaspoon ground cumin
1 teaspoon ground coriander
2 teaspoons turmeric
½ teaspoon cayenne pepper
2 tomatoes – diced
400 ml (14 fl oz) can coconut
    milk
2 tablespoons fish sauce
Juice of ½ a juicy lemon
1 tablespoon sugar
½ cup fresh curry leaves
700 g (1 lb 9 oz) boneless,
    skinless trevally
1 cup peas – defrosted
2 zucchini – cut into ribbons
    using a peeler
A handful of fresh coriander –
    roughly chopped
1 green chilli – finely sliced

Start with cooking the rice as per the packet instructions.

Heat a large deep pan on a medium heat. Add 1 tablespoon of the olive oil and fry the onion with a good pinch of salt for 5 minutes or until it starts to soften. Add the eggplant, garlic and ginger with a further 2 tablespoons of oil. Fry for 2–3 minutes, stirring often.

Add the spices, tomatoes and a quarter of the coconut milk. Stir everything together for a minute or so. Add the remaining coconut milk, along with the fish sauce, lemon juice and sugar. Simmer on low for 10 minutes.

While the sauce is simmering, heat a small pan on a medium/high heat. Add enough oil to cover the bottom of the pan. Add the curry leaves and fry until they are nice and crispy. Gently lift out the crispy leaves and place on a couple of sheets of paper towel. Set aside.

Cut the trevally into 2 cm (¾ in) cubes. Add it to the curry and leave it to simmer away on a low/medium heat for 3–4 minutes or until the fish is just cooked.

Add the peas and zucchini ribbons to the curry. Gently fold everything together for a final 30 seconds. Season with salt and cracked pepper to taste.

Sprinkle the crispy curry leaves, coriander and green chilli (if using) on top, and serve with the steamed basmati rice.

POULTRY

CHICKEN SCHNITZEL WITH A SHAVED FENNEL SALAD

Crumbed chicken is always a failsafe option. Adding parmesan and thyme to the panko mix delivers a welcome flavour hit. I like to throw a few cornichons on top and add a good squeeze of mayonnaise on the side to serve.

SERVES 2

2 x 200 g (7 oz) skinless chicken breasts
⅓ cup flour
1 egg
1½ cups panko crumbs
1 cup finely grated parmesan
1 tablespoon fresh thyme
50 g (1¾ oz) butter
2 tablespoons olive oil

SHAVED FENNEL SALAD

50 g (1¾ oz) spinach leaves – thinly sliced
1 green apple – cut into matchsticks
½ large fennel bulb – thinly sliced with a mandolin
½ cup roughly chopped Italian parsley
1 tablespoon capers
Juice of 1 lemon
1 tablespoon extra virgin olive oil
1 heaped tablespoon mayonnaise (I use Best Foods)

Carefully cut each chicken breast horizontally into two pieces. Place between two sheets of plastic wrap and flatten using a rolling pin or heavy pan.

Put the flour on a shallow plate and season with salt and cracked pepper. Whisk the egg in a bowl. Mix the panko crumbs, parmesan and thyme on a separate plate. Dip the chicken into the flour, then into the egg wash and then into the panko mix, pressing down firmly into the panko crumbs so they stick well. Set aside on a plate.

To make the Shaved Fennel Salad, place the spinach, apple, fennel, parsley and capers in a bowl. Add the lemon juice, olive oil and mayonnaise. Gently toss everything together. Season with salt and cracked pepper.

Heat a large pan on a medium/high heat, then add the butter and oil. Shallow fry the chicken for 2½–3 minutes per side. Serve on two plates with the salad divided up equally.

SOUTH AMERICAN-STYLE SPLAT CHOOK WITH AJI VERDE

Marinating the chicken for as long as possible is seriously worth it. This is also delicious thrown on the barbecue to cook in the warmer months. You can shred the chicken and pop it in a soft tortilla or serve it alongside barbecued corn or the Crispy Golden Kumara Wedges with a Creamy Avocado Tahini Sauce on page 70.

SERVES 4

1.5 kg (3 lb 5 oz) whole
   chicken – butterflied
A handful of fresh coriander

SPICY MARINADE

¼ cup soy sauce
3 tablespoons sriracha
2 tablespoons rice vinegar
1 tablespoon honey
1 tablespoon ground cumin
1 teaspoon paprika
4 large garlic cloves – minced
Zest and juice of 1 lemon

AJI VERDE

2 cups fresh coriander
½ cup thick Greek yoghurt
¼ cup mayonnaise (I use Best
   Foods)
1 large garlic clove
1 green chilli
Juice of 1 lime or lemon

Mix the Spicy Marinade ingredients in a bowl.

Place the chicken skin-side down in a baking dish. Spoon some of the marinade over the underside of the chicken. Gently pull the skin away from the flesh and spoon some of the marinade under the skin.

Cover with plastic wrap. Put in the fridge to marinate for as long as possible, ideally at least an hour.

Pull the chook out of the fridge 20 minutes before cooking so it comes to room temperature.

Preheat the oven to 200°C (400°F) fan bake.

Reposition the chicken skin-side up and spoon the marinade over the chicken. Season with salt and cracked pepper. Roast for 45–55 minutes or until the juices run clear.

While the chicken is cooking, make the Aji Verde by whizzing the ingredients in a blender. Pour into a small serving bowl and set aside.

When the chicken is fully cooked through, set aside to rest for a few minutes before chopping into quarters or eighths. Place the chicken pieces on a serving platter and pour the cooking juices over the top. Garnish with coriander and serve with the Aji Verde.

SPICED CHICKEN WITH A ROAST VEGETABLE ISRAELI COUSCOUS

This recipe is loaded with Middle Eastern flavours, which work perfectly with a dollop of thick Greek yoghurt on the side. I find Alexandra's couscous is best for this dish. There are plenty of other brands, but you might need to adjust the cook time accordingly.

SERVES 4

6 large boneless, skinless
    chicken thighs
2 zucchini – cut into bite-sized
    pieces
1 large eggplant – cut into
    bite-sized pieces
1 red capsicum – cut into bite-
    sized pieces
1 large red onion – quartered
3 tablespoons olive oil
1 tablespoon cumin seeds
1½ cups Israeli couscous
2½ cups chicken stock
¼ cup dried apricots – diced
1 tablespoon ras el hanout
¼ cup roasted pistachios –
    roughly chopped
1 cup chopped fresh parsley
1 cup chopped fresh mint
150 g (5½ oz) feta
⅓ cup pomegranate seeds

CHICKEN MARINADE

2 tablespoons olive oil
1 teaspoon ground cumin
1 teaspoon paprika
1 teaspoon cinnamon
½ teaspoon dried ginger
½ teaspoon turmeric
3 garlic cloves – minced
Juice of 1 lemon

Preheat the oven to 200°C (400°F) fan bake.

In a large bowl, mix the chicken with all the marinade ingredients. Set aside.

Place the zucchini, eggplant, capsicum and onion on a lined baking tray. Drizzle with 2 tablespoons of the olive oil and sprinkle with the cumin seeds. Season with salt and cracked pepper. Place on the lower shelf of the oven and roast for 35–40 minutes.

Heat a medium saucepan on a medium heat. Add the remaining 1 tablespoon of oil. Add the couscous and lightly toast it for a minute. Add the stock, apricots and ras el hanout. Stir well then put the lid on. Simmer on a low/medium heat for 7 minutes, then turn off the heat but leave the lid on and let it sit for 15 minutes.

Place the chicken on a baking tray and season with salt and cracked pepper.

When the vegetables have 20 minutes of cooking time to go, place the chicken on the top shelf of the oven and roast for about 17 minutes or until fully cooked through.

Fold together the couscous and roasted vegetables in a serving bowl. Add the pistachios and half the parsley and mint. Cut the cooked chicken into bite-sized pieces and place on top of the couscous, then sprinkle with chunks of the feta, pomegranate seeds and the remaining parsley and mint.

JAPANESE-INSPIRED CHICKEN SKEWERS WITH CUCUMBER & AVOCADO SALSA

This jazzy little Japanese-inspired recipe harnesses bold flavours that work perfectly with the simple, fresh salad. If using wooden skewers, make sure to soak them in water for at least ten minutes before using them. These are also divine barbecued. For extra flavour, reserve the marinade, heat it up in a pan until bubbling, then pour it over the skewers once cooked. To make zucchini ribbons, use a peeler to cut strips from one side until you reach the middle of the zucchini, then flip and peel the other side. You want the ribbons as wide as possible.

SERVES 3

550 g (1 lb 4 oz) boneless, skinless chicken thighs
150 g (5½ oz) button mushrooms – quartered
White part of 3 spring onions – cut into 2 cm (¾ in) pieces
1 large zucchini – cut into ribbons using a peeler
A drizzle of olive oil

SOY MARINADE

3 tablespoons soy sauce
2½ tablespoons honey
2 tablespoons minced fresh ginger
1½ tablespoons rice wine vinegar
1 tablespoon sesame oil
1 tablespoon chilli oil (plus extra for garnish)
3 large garlic cloves – minced
Zest and juice of 1 lemon

Mix the Soy Marinade ingredients in a large bowl.

Cut the chicken into bite-sized pieces. Add the chicken and mushrooms to the marinade. Set aside to marinate for at least an hour.

Preheat the oven to 200°C (400°F) fan bake.

Start making the skewers, adding the following ingredients in this order: one piece each of chicken, mushroom and spring onion, another piece of chicken, then two folded pieces of zucchini ribbon, followed by one spring onion and one more piece of chicken.

Repeat until all the ingredients have been used up. This should make roughly 12 skewers.

Place the skewers on a lined baking tray. Drizzle with olive oil and season with salt and cracked pepper. Bake for about 15 minutes or until the chicken is fully cooked through (this will vary depending on how big the pieces are).

Ingredients and method continued overleaf

CUCUMBER & AVOCADO SALSA

2 avocados – flesh diced

1 cucumber – cut into 1 cm (½ in) chunks

1 cheek of red onion – finely diced

¼ cup extra virgin olive oil

1½ tablespoons rice wine vinegar

1 tablespoon sugar

Juice of ½ a juicy lemon

⅓ cup roughly chopped fresh coriander (plus extra for garnish)

¼ cup roughly chopped fresh dill

1 teaspoon sesame seeds – toasted (plus extra for garnish)

While the skewers are cooking, make the Cucumber & Avocado Salsa. Place the avocado, cucumber and onion in a serving bowl. Whisk the olive oil, vinegar, sugar and lemon juice in a small bowl, then add to the salad along with the coriander, dill and sesame seeds. Gently fold together.

Once the chicken is fully cooked through, transfer it to a serving platter and drizzle a little extra chilli oil over the top. Garnish with the extra coriander and sesame seeds.

ZA'ATAR & PRESERVED LEMON CHICKEN BAKE

I do love a good tray bake – they are popular because of their ease. Za'atar is one of my favourite spice blends. The yoghurt dressing is so good I could eat it on its own, or lather it over a freshly baked Turkish pide. Team with a side of steamed greens.

SERVES 4-5

8 bone-in, skin-on chicken
    thigh cutlets
3 tablespoons za'atar
2 tablespoons sumac
2 tablespoons honey
5 large garlic cloves – diced
2 quarters preserved lemon –
    finely chopped
1 cup finely chopped Italian
    parsley (plus extra for
    garnish)
1 large golden kumara
1 large fennel bulb
3 tablespoons olive oil

YOGHURT DRESSING

1 cup thick Greek yoghurt
1 tablespoon sumac
1 tablespoon tahini
1 teaspoon water
A squeeze of honey
Juice of ½ a lemon

Preheat the oven to 190°C (375°F) fan bake.

Place the chicken in a large bowl, add 2 tablespoons of the za'atar and 1 tablespoon of the sumac, along with the honey, garlic, preserved lemon and parsley. Season with cracked pepper and turn to coat.

Cut the kumara widthways into 2 cm (¾ in) rounds, then cut in half. Cut away the base of the fennel and discard. Cut the fennel bulb into 1 cm (½ in) pieces.

Place the fennel on a lined baking tray and lay the kumara over the top. Sprinkle with the remaining sumac and za'atar. Season well with salt and cracked pepper. Drizzle with 2 tablespoons of the olive oil.

Place the chicken on a separate baking tray, including all the marinade. Drizzle with the remaining tablespoon of olive oil and season with salt and cracked pepper.

Place the chicken on the lower shelf of the oven and the kumara and fennel on the upper shelf to bake. Remove chicken after 25 minutes or when the juices run clear. Bake kumara and fennel for a further 10 minutes.

While everything is cooking, make the Yoghurt Dressing by mixing the ingredients in a small bowl. Set aside.

When the vegetables and chicken are cooked, smear the Yoghurt Dressing onto a serving platter and arrange the kumara, fennel and chicken on top. Garnish with the extra parsley.

CHILLI COCONUT CHICKEN BAKE

This meal is EASY and devilishly tasty with a good hit of chilli! If you can't get lime, use the juice of a lemon and three whole makrut lime leaves in place of the lime zest.

SERVES 4

1½ cups rice
¼ cup olive oil
8 boneless, skinless chicken thighs
3 garlic cloves – roughly chopped
2 tablespoons minced fresh ginger
1 tablespoon sambal chilli paste
Zest of 2 limes
Juice of 1 lime
2 tablespoons sugar
400 ml (14 fl oz) can coconut milk
250 g (9 oz) broccolini – halved
1 large zucchini – cut into ribbons using a peeler
1 cup roughly chopped fresh coriander

TO SERVE

Lime wedges
½ red chilli – thinly sliced
1 spring onion – thinly sliced

Preheat the oven to 180°C (350°F) fan bake.

Get the rice cooking as per the packet instructions.

Heat a large pan on a high heat. Add 2 tablespoons of the olive oil. Season the chicken with salt and cracked pepper. When the pan is hot, sear the chicken pieces for 1 minute per side and then set aside on a plate.

Heat a deep ovenproof pan on a medium heat. Add the remaining 2 tablespoons of oil, then add the garlic, ginger, chilli paste, lime zest and lime juice. Stir in the sugar and coconut milk, cook for 1 minute then add the chicken. Place the pan, uncovered, in the oven for 20 minutes.

Take the pan out of the oven and add the broccolini in the gaps between the chicken pieces. Put the pan back in the oven and bake for a further 3 minutes or until the chicken is fully cooked through.

Stir in the zucchini ribbons and coriander, reserving a handful of coriander for garnish if desired. Serve with the steamed rice, lime wedges, chilli and spring onion.

MISO CHICKEN & RICE BAKE

A great meal to serve when you have a few people coming for dinner, this one-pot dish tastes like heaven yet is fuss-free to make. It is important to use white miso paste if you can, as it's far less salty than its brown counterpart. Serve with pan-fried broccoli and bok choy on the side.

SERVES 4

6 large bone-in, skin-on
    chicken thigh cutlets
1½ cups white rice
2 cups chicken stock
1 cup water
½ white onion – finely diced
A sprinkling of sesame seeds –
    toasted
A handful of fresh coriander
½ red chilli – thinly sliced

MISO MARINADE

⅓ cup white miso paste
    (or ¼ cup brown miso)
3 tablespoons honey
2 tablespoons soy sauce
2 tablespoons mirin
2 tablespoons minced fresh
    ginger
3 large garlic cloves – minced
1 teaspoon chilli flakes
¼ teaspoon white pepper

SESAME MAYO

½ cup mayonnaise (I use
    Kewpie)
1 tablespoon soy sauce
2 teaspoons sesame oil

Preheat the oven to 200°C (400°F) fan bake.

Mix the Miso Marinade ingredients in a large bowl. Trim any excess skin off the chicken. Add the chicken to the marinade, stirring to make sure it is well coated.

Pour the rice into a large baking dish. Mix in the stock, water and onion. Gently place the chicken pieces on top, pouring all the marinating juices on too. Cover with a lid or 2 layers of tin foil. Bake for 30 minutes.

While the chicken is cooking, make the Sesame Mayo by mixing the ingredients in a bowl. Set aside.

When the chicken has cooked for 30 minutes, take the baking dish out of the oven, working quickly to keep the heat in the oven. Carefully remove the lid or tin foil, then pop the dish back in the oven uncovered for a further 25 minutes or until the chicken is fully cooked through.

Serve in the baking dish, drizzled with the Sesame Mayo and garnished with sesame seeds, coriander and chilli.

THE ULTIMATE TOMATO CHICKEN TRAY BAKE

This beautiful meal is ideally accompanied by either garlic bread or mashed or roasted potato (to mop up that mouth-watering sauce). Add a bottle of wine, a simple green salad and good company.

SERVES 4-5

2 tablespoons olive oil
1 large brown onion – diced
250 g (9 oz) button mushrooms – quartered
1 red capsicum – diced
5 large garlic cloves – roughly chopped
1 teaspoon chilli flakes
2 tablespoons fresh thyme
1½ tablespoons very finely chopped fresh rosemary
½ cup red wine
400 g (14 oz) can crushed tomatoes
3 tablespoons tomato paste
½ cup green olives – pitted
2 tablespoons capers
8 boneless, skinless chicken thighs
100 g (3½ oz) feta – broken into chunks
A handful of Italian parsley – roughly chopped

Preheat the oven to 180°C (350°F) fan bake.

Heat a large ovenproof pan on a low/medium heat. Add 1 tablespoon of the olive oil, then add the onion and a good pinch of salt. Cook for 5 minutes or until the onion is soft, stirring occasionally.

Add the mushrooms, capsicum, garlic, chilli, thyme and rosemary with a splash more oil. Simmer for a couple of minutes, stirring occasionally.

Pour the wine into the pan and let it simmer for a minute. Add the crushed tomatoes, tomato paste, olives and capers. Stir well then fold in the chicken. Cover the dish with a lid or tin foil and bake for 20 minutes.

Take the dish out of the oven, remove the lid or tin foil, sprinkle with the chunks of feta and place back in the oven uncovered for another 25 minutes until the chicken is beautifully cooked. Garnish with the parsley.

HARISSA OLIVE CHICKEN WITH ROASTED KUMARA

This is a two-tray-bake kind of meal, which means a low-maintenance dinner packed with flavour. Harissa paste is a constant saviour in my household — throw it onto basically anything and your meal is elevated in taste about 110 per cent.

SERVES 4

800 g (1 lb 12 oz) boneless, skinless chicken thighs
⅓ cup green olives – pitted
⅓ cup harissa paste
Juice of 1 lemon
¼ cup olive oil
2 large golden kumara
1 large red onion – cut into 8 wedges
5 garlic cloves – skin on, tops trimmed
2 tablespoons pumpkin seeds
1 tablespoon cumin seeds
A handful of Italian parsley or dill – roughly chopped

YOGHURT SAUCE

1 cup thick Greek yoghurt
1 tablespoon chilli oil
1 cup very finely chopped Italian parsley
Juice of 1 lemon

Preheat the oven to 200°C (400°F) fan bake.

Mix the chicken, olives, harissa, lemon juice and 2 tablespoons of the olive oil in a large bowl.

Cut the kumara into 2 cm (¾ in) slices. Place on a lined baking tray with the onion and garlic. Drizzle with the remaining 2 tablespoons of olive oil. Season with salt and cracked pepper. Add the pumpkin seeds and cumin. Place on the lower shelf of the oven and roast for 40 minutes.

After the kumara has been cooking for 25 minutes, transfer the chicken to a lined baking tray. Working quickly to keep the heat in the oven, remove the garlic from the kumara tray and place the chicken on the top shelf of the oven. Cook for 15–20 minutes (depending on size) until fully cooked through.

To make the Yoghurt Sauce, mix the ingredients in a bowl. Season with salt and cracked pepper. Set aside.

Smear the Yoghurt Sauce onto the base of a serving platter, then add the kumara and onion and all their seedy goodness. Squeeze the roasted garlic cloves out of their skins and then top with the chicken and olives and garnish with parsley or dill.

THAI-INSPIRED CHICKEN QUINOA SALAD

When I was growing up, my mum used sweet chilli a lot in her cooking and, my goodness, did I lap it up. This is a healthier spin on the chicken, sweet chilli and orzo pasta she used to make.

SERVES 4

6 large boneless, skinless chicken thighs
1 cup quinoa
2 tablespoons light cooking oil
1 cup peas
4 baby cucumbers – diced
1 red capsicum – thinly sliced into matchsticks
1 large avocado – flesh sliced
½ large mango – flesh thinly sliced
½ punnet cherry tomatoes – halved
½ small red onion – thinly sliced
1 cup chopped fresh mint
1 cup chopped fresh coriander (plus extra leaves for garnish)
⅓ cup roasted cashews – roughly chopped
1 large lime – sliced into wedges

THAI MARINADE

⅓ cup sweet chilli sauce
1 tablespoon soy sauce
1 tablespoon sriracha
2 tablespoons fish sauce
Zest and juice of 1 lime
2 large garlic cloves – minced
1 tablespoon minced fresh ginger

To make the Thai Marinade, combine the ingredients in a large bowl. Add the chicken, making sure it is well coated. Set aside to marinate for at least half an hour or longer if you have time.

Get the quinoa cooking as per the packet instructions. When cooked, set aside to cool.

Preheat the oven to 200°C (400°F) fan bake.

Heat the oil in a pan on a medium/high heat. When you start to see wisps of smoke, brown the chicken. Working in batches, sear the chicken on both sides (roughly 40 seconds per side), then place on a lined baking tray. Pour the remaining marinade over the top and bake for 13–15 minutes (depending on size) until the chicken is fully cooked through.

Defrost the peas by running them under hot water and drying them on paper towels. Place in a large mixing bowl with the cucumber, capsicum, avocado, mango, cherry tomatoes, onion, mint and coriander. Add the cooled quinoa and toss gently. Transfer to a serving platter and set aside.

When the chicken is done, let it cool for a few minutes. Cut into roughly 2 cm (¾ in) slices and place on a separate serving plate. Pour half the marinade juices from the baking dish over the quinoa salad and the rest over the chicken.

Gently toss the salad. Top with cashews and a few extra coriander leaves. Scatter a few sprigs of coriander over the chicken and serve with the lime wedges.

SOUTH-EAST ASIAN CHICKEN BOWL WITH A MANGO SALSA

I could eat this meal once a week and never ever get sick of it. The flavour of the chilli sauce will absolutely knock your socks off (and I encourage you to use it on beef, pork and seafood going forward).

SERVES 3

1 cup brown rice
2 skin-on chicken breasts
1 tablespoon light cooking oil

MANGO SALSA

1 zucchini – julienned
1 mango – flesh diced
1 avocado – flesh diced
1 red capsicum – finely diced
A handful of fresh coriander
A splash of chilli oil
Juice of ½ a lemon

CHILLI DIPPING SAUCE

¼ cup fish sauce
¼ cup lime juice
1 shallot – thinly sliced
1 large red chilli – finely diced
1½ tablespoons sugar
½ teaspoon chilli flakes
1 tablespoon diced coriander
　stalks

Preheat the oven to 200°C (400°F) fan bake.

Get the rice cooking as per the packet instructions.

To make the Mango Salsa, combine the ingredients in a bowl. Season with cracked pepper. Set aside in the fridge.

Season the chicken with salt and cracked pepper. Heat the oil in a pan over a high heat and sear the chicken on both sides until browned. Place skin-side up on a lined baking tray. Roast for 15-17 minutes (depending on size) until cooked through.

To make the Chilli Dipping Sauce, mix the ingredients in a small bowl.

When the chicken is cooked, cover it with tin foil and let it sit for 3 minutes, then carve it against the grain into 2 cm (¾ in) slices.

Divide the rice between three bowls, then do the same with the Mango Salsa and sliced chicken. Top with the Chilli Dipping Sauce.

CHINESE DUCK NOODLE STIR-FRY

Here, slow-cooking the duck ensures the meat is nice and tender. Once the duck is cooked, this stir-fry is very quick to throw together. Make sure you are well prepped before you start frying — ingredients sliced, sauces ready and water boiling for the noodles. A duck maryland is the thigh and drumstick in one piece (with the bone in).

SERVES 4

4 duck marylands
1½ teaspoons Chinese five spice
500 g (1 lb 2 oz) fresh egg noodles
1 tablespoon light cooking oil
1 tablespoon chilli oil
3 large spring onions – cut into 1 cm (½ in) pieces
3 garlic cloves – diced
2 tablespoons minced fresh ginger
2 large heads bok choy
1 cup peas
⅓ cup roasted cashews – roughly chopped
½ red chilli – thinly sliced
A handful of fresh coriander – roughly chopped
½ lime – cut into wedges

STIR-FRY SAUCE

3 tablespoons soy sauce
1 tablespoon Chinkiang vinegar
3 tablespoons hoisin sauce
2 teaspoons sesame oil
Juice of ½ a lime
½ teaspoon white pepper

Preheat the oven to 160°C (315°F) fan bake.

Trim any excess skin off the duck marylands and place on a lined baking tray. Sprinkle on both sides with the five spice and season with salt. Cover loosely with tin foil and roast for 45 minutes. Remove foil and roast for a further 35–40 minutes.

When the duck has 10 minutes of cooking time remaining, heat a large saucepan of boiling water on a high heat. Add the noodles and cook as per the packet instructions. Drain well and set aside.

Make the Stir-fry Sauce by mixing the ingredients in a small bowl. Set aside.

Take the duck out of the oven. Using a couple of forks, carefully pull the meat off the bones. Chop the skin into smaller pieces. Cover with tin foil and set aside.

Heat a large wok on a low heat. Add the oil and chilli oil, then the spring onions, garlic and ginger. Cook gently for 5 minutes, stirring often.

While the spring onions are cooking, trim off the bases of the bok choy and cut the leaves crossways into 1 cm (½ in) slices. Turn up the heat and add the bok choy, stirring for 30 seconds. Add the peas and cook for 1 minute, stirring often. Add the drained noodles and shredded duck.

Add the Stir-fry Sauce to the wok. Working quickly, using a spatula and tongs, toss everything together for a minute or so. Garnish with cashews, chilli, coriander and lime wedges.

MEAT

TAMARIND COCONUT BEEF CURRY WITH SPRING ONION FLATBREADS

I love this warming, zingy curry. Cross-cut beef is my new favourite cut to slow-cook — the fat becomes so tender and the meat so soft. The Spring Onion Flatbreads are perfect for mopping up the sauce.

SERVES 6

1.2 kg (3 lb 2 oz) cross-cut beef
3 tablespoons light cooking oil
1 brown onion – diced
⅓ cup finely diced fresh ginger
3 large garlic cloves – diced
1⅓ cups beef stock
½ cup tamarind purée/paste
½ cup honey
2 tablespoons sesame oil
2 tablespoons ground cumin
1 teaspoon chilli flakes
3 large makrut lime leaves – whole
400 ml (14 fl oz) can coconut cream
1½ cups white rice
½ cup roughly chopped fresh coriander
1 red chilli – thinly sliced
A dollop of sour cream

SPRING ONION FLATBREADS

1 cup flour
1 teaspoon baking powder
100 g (3½ oz) thick Greek yoghurt
½ cup thinly sliced spring onion
1½ teaspoons sesame oil
1½ teaspoons olive oil
Oil, for frying

Preheat the oven to 150°C (300°F) fan bake.

Cut the beef into 3 cm (1¼ in) chunks, leaving the fat on. Season with salt and cracked pepper. Set aside.

Heat a large saucepan on a low/medium heat. Add 2 tablespoons of the oil. Add the onion, ginger and garlic and fry for a couple of minutes, stirring occasionally. Season with salt and cracked pepper.

Add the stock, tamarind, honey, sesame oil, cumin, chilli flakes and lime leaves. Add the coconut cream then fill the can quarter full with water, swirl it around and pour it into the curry. Stir, then leave to simmer on a low heat.

Heat a separate pan on a high heat. Add the remaining tablespoon of oil. Working in batches, and adding more oil if necessary, sear the beef until browned.

Transfer the beef to a medium-sized deep baking dish. Add the tamarind sauce, cover with a lid or 2 layers of tin foil and bake for 3 hours until the beef is falling apart.

When the beef has 1½ hours cooking time to go, make the Spring Onion Flatbreads. Mix the flour and baking powder in a large bowl. Make a well in the middle, add the yoghurt and spring onion and mix until the dough is nicely formed. Add the sesame oil and olive oil and knead the dough for a few more minutes.

Place dough in the bowl, cover with plastic wrap and put in the fridge for 1 hour.

Continued overleaf

Half an hour before the beef is ready, cook the rice as per the packet instructions. When cooked, leave it to sit with the lid on.

To cook the Spring Onion Flatbreads, cut the dough into 6 pieces, then roll each piece out into a 12 cm (4½ in) circle. When the beef is just about cooked, heat a large pan on a medium heat. Add a generous tablespoon of oil and fry the flatbreads in batches until crispy on both sides. Set aside on a plate.

Remove the lime leaves from the baking dish and discard them. Scatter the coriander and chilli over the beef in the dish. Serve in the dish, accompanied with the steamed rice, flatbreads and a big dollop of sour cream.

EYE FILLET ON A CREAMY BUTTER BEAN SPINACH SITUATION

In this recipe I've partnered juicy steaks with a tasty and ever-so-slightly creamy butter bean accompaniment. You could also roast a whole eye fillet, double the butter bean recipe and serve it for a larger group.

SERVES 4

4 x 180 g (6 oz) eye fillet steaks
A little olive oil, to drizzle

CREAMY BUTTER BEAN SPINACH

2½ tablespoons olive oil
1 brown onion – diced
1 leek – thinly sliced
3 garlic cloves – diced
2 tablespoons fresh thyme
⅓ cup white wine
2 tablespoons capers
2 tablespoons Dijon mustard
400 g (14 oz) can butter
    beans – drained and rinsed
150 g (5½ oz) spinach leaves –
    roughly chopped
Juice of 1 lemon
¼ cup crème fraîche
A big handful of Italian
    parsley – roughly chopped

To make the Creamy Butter Bean Spinach, heat a large pan on a low/medium heat. Add 2 tablespoons of the oil, then the onion, leek, garlic and thyme. Cook for 7 minutes until soft then turn off the heat.

Heat a cast iron pan on a hot heat. Season the steaks with salt and cracked pepper and drizzle with olive oil. Fry the steaks for 2–3 minutes per side (depending on their size). Transfer to a plate, loosely cover with tin foil and set aside to rest for 5 minutes.

While the steak is resting, return the pan with the onion mixture to a medium heat and add the remaining ½ tablespoon of oil, along with the wine, capers and mustard. Simmer for a couple of minutes, stirring from time to time.

Fold in the butter beans, stirring for about a minute. Gently fold in the spinach, squeezing the lemon juice over the top. Season with cracked pepper. Once the spinach starts to wilt, fold in the crème fraîche and parsley.

By this time the steak should be well rested. Slice the steak and serve on top of this divine little creation.

JAPANESE-STYLE STEAK TACOS

My dear friend Richard introduced me to Japanese steak tacos. With a few tweaks, these have been a staple in my house ever since. They're truly simple and the Wasabi Mayo is an addictive condiment!

SERVES 4

750 g (1 lb 10 oz) skirt steak
1 large avocado – flesh sliced
¼ purple cabbage – very finely sliced or shaved
A handful of fresh coriander
Lime wedges
1 tablespoon light cooking oil
10 mini soft tortillas
½ red chilli – thinly sliced (optional)

JAPANESE MARINADE

2½ tablespoons white miso paste
2½ tablespoons mirin
1½ tablespoons sesame oil
1½ tablespoons sugar

QUICK CUCUMBER PICKLE

5 tablespoons rice wine vinegar
1½ tablespoons caster sugar
1 Lebanese cucumber – thinly sliced
½ red onion – thinly sliced

WASABI MAYO

1 cup mayonnaise (I use Kewpie)
1 tablespoon wasabi (or more if you want it spicy)

Combine the marinade ingredients in a bowl. Add the steak, coating it well. Season with lots of cracked pepper. Leave to marinate for at least 30 minutes.

To make the Quick Cucumber Pickle, mix the vinegar and sugar in a medium bowl, stirring until the sugar has dissolved. Add the cucumber and onion. Stir well to make sure they are well coated. Season with salt. Set aside to pickle for 20 minutes.

To make the Wasabi Mayo, combine the ingredients in a small serving bowl, increasing the amount of wasabi until you are satisfied with the heat/taste. Set aside.

Divide the avocado, cabbage, coriander and lime wedges between individual serving bowls or plates. Set aside.

Heat a cast iron pan on a medium/high heat. Add 1 tablespoon of oil. When you start to see wisps of smoke, fry the steak for 2–3 minutes per side (or longer, depending on thickness), until cooked to your liking. Transfer to a board, loosely cover with tin foil and set aside to rest for a couple of minutes.

While the steak is resting, fry the tortillas over a gas flame or in a pan. Fold them in half and put them on a serving plate.

Drain the pickle juice from the cucumbers and onion and put them into a small serving bowl.

Carve the steak into thin slices against the grain (this is very important). Arrange on a serving board. Serve accompanied by the Quick Cucumber Pickle, Wasabi Mayo, tortillas and chilli (if using). Let everyone help themselves.

BEEF & RICOTTA MEATBALL PASTA

There is something so comforting about meatballs. These are packed with flavour and ever so slightly cheesy, so each one is a delicious morsel.

SERVES 5

500 g (1 lb 2 oz) dried
    spaghetti
2 tablespoons olive oil
½ cup chopped Italian parsley
2 zucchini – cut into ribbons
    using a peeler
Shaved parmesan
Fresh basil

BEEF & RICOTTA MEATBALLS

500 g (1 lb 2 oz) prime beef
    mince
½ cup panko crumbs
½ cup ricotta
¼ cup grated parmesan
1 large egg
3 tablespoons pine nuts –
    toasted
1 tablespoon Dijon mustard
1 tablespoon dried oregano
1 garlic clove – minced
Zest of 1 lemon
Oil, for frying

TOMATO PASTA SAUCE

1 tablespoon olive oil
A knob of butter
1 brown onion – finely diced
4 garlic cloves – diced
1 teaspoon chilli flakes
1 teaspoon dried oregano
2 x 400 g (14 oz) cans whole
    tomatoes
1 tablespoon balsamic vinegar
1 teaspoon sugar

To make the Beef & Ricotta Meatballs, mix the ingredients in a bowl. Season with salt and cracked pepper. Roll into 20 balls and set aside.

To make the Tomato Pasta Sauce, heat a large, deep pan on a low/medium heat. Add the olive oil and butter. Add the onion and a pinch of salt and cook for 5 minutes, stirring often, until the onion is soft. Don't let it brown.

Stir in the garlic, chilli and oregano and cook for a further 5 minutes, stirring occasionally. Add the canned tomatoes, then add a splash of water to each can, swirl it around and pour it into the sauce. Stir in the balsamic vinegar and sugar. Leave the sauce to simmer away.

Bring a large saucepan of generously salted water to the boil on a high heat.

Once the sauce is simmering, add the pasta to the boiling water and cook as per the packet instructions.

To cook the meatballs, heat a separate pan on a medium/high heat. Add 2 tablespoons of olive oil. Fry the meatballs in batches for 3 minutes per side (6 minutes in total). Once the meatballs are cooked, add them to the pasta sauce.

Drain the pasta, reserving ½ cup of pasta water.

Stir the parsley through the pasta sauce, then gently fold in the spaghetti and zucchini ribbons, adding a splash of reserved pasta water if required. Serve immediately with lots of parmesan and basil.

DAN DAN NOODLES

I am going to put it out there and say this is the best stir-fry I've made. Whoever you're making it for will absolutely lose their gherkin. It's spicy, but if you don't like spice or if you're using a very hot chilli oil, just adjust the amount accordingly.

SERVES 4

1 tablespoon olive oil
400 g (14 oz) beef mince
¼ teaspoon Chinese five spice
500 g (1 lb 2 oz) fresh noodles
    (I use Lian Huat)
1 tablespoon soy sauce
1 tablespoon Chinkiang
    vinegar
1 heaped tablespoon hoisin
    sauce
2 large heads bok choy
Green part of 2 spring onions –
    thinly sliced
Chilli oil, to taste (I use
    Tsunami Mami)

DAN DAN SAUCE

⅓ cup chilli oil (I use Tsunami
    Mami)
3 tablespoons soy sauce
1 tablespoon Chinkiang
    vinegar
1 tablespoon crunchy peanut
    butter
1 tablespoon tahini paste
1 teaspoon sesame oil
½ teaspoon Sichuan dried
    pepper
3 garlic cloves – minced

To make the Dan Dan Sauce, mix the ingredients in a bowl. Set aside.

Bring a large saucepan of water to the boil on a high heat.

Heat a wok on a high heat. Add the olive oil. Add the mince and five spice and cook, stirring, until evenly browned.

Add the noodles to the boiling water and cook as per the packet instructions.

Once the mince is nearly cooked, add the soy, vinegar and hoisin, stirring well. Turn the heat to low.

Trim off the base of the bok choy and cut the leaves in half lengthways.

When the noodles have 1 minute to go, add the bok choy. Drain the noodles and bok choy and add them to the wok. Turn up the heat and add the Dan Dan Sauce. Stir everything together for a couple of minutes until the noodles are well coated with the sauce. Top with the spring onions and extra chilli oil. Serve immediately.

LAMB RUMP WITH POMEGRANATE SALSA & SOFT ROASTED EGGPLANT

This is a summery delight that I absolutely adore. Serve with toasted pita pockets or roasted potatoes and a big glass of red wine.

SERVES 4

About ½ cup olive oil
1 tablespoon dried oregano
2 large garlic cloves – minced
4 x 200 g (7 oz) lamb rumps
2 large eggplants
A big handful of baby rocket leaves

POMEGRANATE SALSA

⅓ cup extra virgin olive oil
1 teaspoon sugar
Zest of 1 lemon
Juice of 1 juicy lemon
½ cup pomegranate seeds
⅓ cup roasted pistachios – roughly chopped
1 cup finely chopped Italian parsley
¼ cup finely chopped fresh oregano

YOGHURT FETA WHIP

3 garlic cloves
1 cup thick Greek yoghurt
100 g (3½ oz) cow's milk feta
1 tablespoon extra virgin olive oil
1 tablespoon honey
Juice of 1 lemon

Preheat the oven to 200°C (400°F) fan bake.

Mix 2 tablespoons of the olive oil with the oregano and garlic in a bowl. Add the lamb rumps, mixing well so the lamb is coated. Season with cracked pepper and set aside.

Slice the eggplants into 1.5 cm (⅝ in) rounds. Cut the tops off the 3 garlic cloves for the Yoghurt Feta Whip, keeping the skin on.

Place the eggplant slices and garlic cloves on a lined baking tray, drizzle with ¼ cup of the olive oil and season with salt and cracked pepper. Roast for 35–40 minutes on the lower shelf of the oven.

To make the Pomegranate Salsa, place the olive oil, sugar, lemon zest and lemon juice in a bowl and whisk with a fork. Season with salt and cracked pepper. Add the pomegranate seeds, pistachios, parsley and oregano. Set aside.

When the eggplant has been cooking for 15 minutes, heat a medium pan over a medium/high heat. Add 1 tablespoon of olive oil and when it is starting to smoke, sear the lamb for 1½ minutes on each side until browned. Place the lamb on a baking tray. Roast for about 13 minutes.

Remove the lamb and garlic cloves from the oven. Cover the lamb with tin foil and set aside to rest for 10 minutes.

To make the Yoghurt Feta Whip, squeeze the roasted garlic cloves out of their skins into a food processor or blender. Add the yoghurt, feta, olive oil, honey and lemon juice and blitz until smooth.

Continued overleaf

Remove the eggplant from the oven. Carve the rested lamb against the grain (this is very important) into roughly 1 cm (½ in) slices.

Spread the Yoghurt Feta Whip onto the base of a large serving platter. Add the eggplant, rocket and sliced lamb, and top with half the beautiful Pomegranate Salsa, reserving half in a ramekin for the table.

LAMB MEATBALLS WITH GREMOLATA & A PUMPKIN WHIP

I remember the first time I made this, I couldn't quite comprehend how tasty it was. If you like lamb, look no further. There are so many beautiful flavours — it's a total sensation!

SERVES 4

1.2 kg (2 lb 10 oz) pumpkin
3 tablespoons olive oil
1 teaspoon dukkah
100 g (3½ oz) feta
¼ cup thick Greek yoghurt
1 tablespoon extra virgin olive oil
Juice of ½ a lemon

SPICED LAMB MEATBALLS

800 g (1 lb 12 oz) lamb mince
1½ cups breadcrumbs
2 eggs
1 large brown onion – very finely diced
4 garlic cloves – minced
2 teaspoons allspice
1 teaspoon cinnamon
1½ cups finely chopped Italian parsley

PARSLEY & CORIANDER GREMOLATA

½ cup extra virgin olive oil
1 garlic clove
1½ cups fresh Italian parsley
1 cup fresh coriander
Zest of 1 large lemon
Juice of 1 juicy lemon

Preheat the oven to 180°C (350°F) fan bake.

Cut the skin off the pumpkin and discard the seeds. Chop the flesh into roughly 4 cm (1½ in) chunks. Place on a lined baking tray, drizzle with 2 tablespoons of the oil and sprinkle with the dukkah. Season with salt and cracked pepper. Roast for 40 minutes or until soft.

While the pumpkin is roasting, make the Spiced Lamb Meatballs by mixing the ingredients in a bowl, seasoning with salt and cracked pepper and rolling into golf ball-sized balls. Set aside.

To make the Parsley & Coriander Gremolata, blitz the ingredients in a food processor until smooth. Season with salt and cracked pepper. Set aside in a ramekin.

Turn the oven up to 200°C (400°F).

Heat a large pan on a high heat. Add the remaining tablespoon of oil. Sear the meatballs on two sides for roughly 45 seconds per side. Place the seared meatballs on a baking tray and bake for roughly 7 minutes.

By this time the pumpkin should be cooked. Transfer it to a food processor with the feta, yoghurt, extra virgin olive oil and lemon juice and blend to a purée. Spoon evenly onto four plates, add the meatballs then top with the gremolata.

BARBECUE LAMB WITH CHIMICHURRI & CHARRED BABY COS

If left to my own devices, I would put Chimichurri on practically everything. I recommend making a double batch and keeping half in the fridge to use later in the week for a different meal. Serve this with a side of garlic bread.

SERVES 5

1.2 kg (2 lb 10 oz) butterflied lamb leg
A drizzle of olive oil

CHIMICHURRI

2 cups firmly packed Italian parsley
½ cup extra virgin olive oil
1 tablespoon red wine vinegar
2 teaspoons dried oregano
1 teaspoon honey
¼ teaspoon smoked paprika
1 large garlic clove
Juice of ½ a large lemon

CHARRED BABY COS

2 baby cos lettuces
2 tablespoons olive oil
Juice of 1 large juicy lemon
⅓ cup finely grated parmesan

To make the Chimichurri, blitz the ingredients in a food processor until smooth, then season to taste. Set aside.

Bring the lamb leg to room temperature. Drizzle with a little olive oil and season with salt and cracked pepper on both sides.

Preheat the barbecue on high. Sear the lamb for 4 minutes each side, then turn the heat to medium, close the lid and cook for a further 10 minutes or until the internal temperature reaches 54°C (130°F) for medium cooked lamb. Put it on a plate, cover it with tin foil and set it aside to rest for 10 minutes. Turn the barbecue to hot.

While the lamb is resting, make the Charred Baby Cos. Cut the baby cos lettuces in half lengthways. Whisk the olive oil and lemon juice in a bowl with salt and cracked pepper and brush onto both sides of the lettuce halves. Barbecue for 4 minutes flat-side down, then flip and cook for a further 2 minutes. Cut each in half again, arrange on a large serving platter and top with parmesan.

Carve the lamb across the grain and arrange it on the serving platter. Drizzle some of the Chimichurri over the top and serve the rest in a ramekin.

SLOW-COOKED HARISSA LAMB SHOULDER

This was one of the original recipes on my MPK Instagram page, and would have to be one of my favourites in this book. The harissa glaze is a sure way to jazz up your next Sunday roast. Try it with couscous or crispy potatoes.

SERVES 6

2 kg (4 lb 8 oz) bone-in lamb shoulder
5 garlic cloves – halved lengthways
¼ cup harissa paste
3¼ cups vegetable stock
A handful of fresh parsley
A handful of fresh coriander

CHILLI ORANGE GLAZE

½ cup fresh orange juice
¼ cup harissa paste
¼ cup honey
1 large red chilli – thinly sliced

Preheat the oven to 150°C (300°F) fan bake.

Cut 10 small holes into the lamb and poke the garlic into the holes. Rub the lamb with the harissa paste. Season with salt and cracked pepper. Place in a deep baking dish and pour the stock around the edges (don't pour it over the lamb as you will wash off the seasoning). Cover with a lid or 2 layers of tin foil and bake for 4½–5 hours until the lamb is juicy and falling apart.

When there are 20 minutes of cooking time to go, make the Chilli Orange Glaze by heating a small saucepan on a medium heat, adding the ingredients, mixing and simmering for 5 minutes.

When the lamb is cooked, take it out of the oven. Turn the oven up to 200°C (400°F) fan bake.

Remove the lid or tin foil and gently pour a third of the Chilli Orange Glaze over the lamb. Place the lamb back in the oven for 10 minutes uncovered.

Remove the lamb from the oven, loosely cover with foil and set aside to rest for 10 minutes.

Once rested, carefully transfer the lamb to a serving platter and gently pull the meat apart. I like to pour over some of the pan juices, then finish by pouring over the rest of the glaze. Garnish with the parsley and coriander.

CRISPY PORK BELLY WITH A CREAMY RED CURRY

At first glance this might look complicated, but it is actually a rather simple curry sauce. Whenever I make it, I also like to mix some really hot chopped red chilli with fish sauce and serve it on the side in a little ramekin as a flavour enhancer — I call it my spicy elixir. I promise, it will knock the socks off your guests (in a good way).

SERVES 4–5

1 kg (2 lb 4 oz) pork belly
1 teaspoon salt
400 ml (14 fl oz) can coconut milk
1 cup vegetable stock
1½ cups jasmine rice

CREAMY RED CURRY SAUCE

3 tablespoons vegetable oil
1 large red onion – halved and thinly sliced
2 tablespoons minced fresh ginger
4 garlic cloves – roughly chopped
195 g (7 oz) jar red curry paste (I use Ayam)
2 heaped tablespoons peanut butter
3 makrut lime leaves – whole
400 ml (14 fl oz) coconut milk
1 tablespoon sugar
2 large heads bok choy
1½ tablespoons fish sauce
½ cup chopped fresh coriander

Preheat the oven to 230°C (450°F) fan bake.

Score the skin of the pork with a very sharp knife, being careful not to cut through to the meat. Pat the pork dry with paper towels. Rub the skin with the salt. Place the pork skin-side up in a small baking dish. Place on the top shelf of the oven and roast for 20 minutes.

Remove the pork from the oven. Turn the oven down to 160°C (315°F) fan bake. Carefully pour the coconut milk and stock around the pork. Do not let the liquid touch any of the skin. Carefully place back into the oven and cook for 1½ hours.

When the pork has 30 minutes of cooking time left, cook the rice as per the packet instructions.

To make the Creamy Red Curry Sauce, heat a large saucepan on a medium heat. Add the oil. Gently fry the onion and ginger for 5 minutes. Stir in the garlic, curry paste, peanut butter, lime leaves and half the coconut milk. Simmer for 2 minutes. Add the remaining coconut milk and the sugar. Turn the temperature to low/medium and simmer for 15 minutes.

By now the pork should be cooked. Turn the oven to the grill setting to crisp the pork crackling. This could take roughly 5 minutes but keep a very close eye on it! Once it has crackled to your liking, remove it from the oven. Set aside.

Continued overleaf

Trim off the base of the bok choy and cut the leaves in half lengthways. Stir the bok choy, fish sauce and half the coriander into the curry sauce.

Carefully place the pork crackling-side down on a chopping board. Cut it into 4–5 pieces.

Evenly distribute the rice between serving bowls. Place the pork on top, crackling-side up. Using tongs, remove the lime leaves from the curry sauce and discard them, then lift the bok choy out of the sauce and place it into the bowls next to the pork.

Carefully pour the curry sauce around the pork and garnish with the remaining coriander.

PORK LOIN WITH AN ASIAN CHILLI, GINGER & PEAR SAUCE

This recipe was inspired by a dessert (of all things) that Peter Gordon made at an event I attended. I thought the ginger and pear combo would be incredible on pork, and I promise you it is! Enjoy with some crunchy steamed broccoli or a big salad.

SERVES 4

2 x 400 g (14 oz) pork loin
    fillets
3 tablespoons olive oil
2 large golden kumara
50 g (1¾ oz) butter
A handful of fresh coriander
1 red chilli – thinly sliced
    (optional)

CHILLI, GINGER & PEAR SAUCE

4 large pears
2 lemons
1 cup caster sugar
½ cup finely diced fresh ginger
1 teaspoon chilli flakes
¼ teaspoon sea salt

Bring the pork to room temperature for an hour.

Place the pork on a plate, drizzle with 1 tablespoon of the olive oil and season with salt and cracked pepper. Set aside.

Bring a large saucepan of salted water to the boil on a medium/high heat. Peel the kumara and cut into medium chunks. Boil for 12–15 minutes or until soft.

While the kumara is boiling, make the Chilli, Ginger & Pear Sauce. Peel the pears, then chop them into 1 cm (½ in) chunks. Zest the two lemons over the chopped pears and set aside. Juice the lemons into a bowl. Place the sugar in a non-stick pan and dry cook it on a low/medium heat until it caramelises. Shake the pan often to move the sugar around, but do not stir . . . as tempting as it is. Be sure to keep an eye on it so it doesn't burn. This should take roughly 10 minutes.

When the sugar has just started to caramelise and there are no clumps left, add the ginger, chilli and salt. It will sizzle for a bit. Quickly add the pear, lemon zest and lemon juice. Using a non-stick utensil, stir until well combined. Simmer for 20 minutes on a low/medium heat, stirring occasionally.

While the sauce is simmering, add the remaining 2 tablespoons of olive oil to a pan on a medium/high heat. Cook the pork for 3 minutes on all four sides (12 minutes in total). Wrap in tin foil and set aside to rest for 10 minutes.

Continued overleaf

Drain the kumara well. Return it to the saucepan, add the butter and season with salt and cracked pepper. Mash until smooth. Put the lid on to keep warm and set aside.

Carve the pork into 2 cm (¾ in) slices. Divide the mash between the four serving plates, then place the sliced pork next to the mash. Spoon the Chilli, Ginger & Pear Sauce on top of the pork and garnish with the coriander and chilli (if using).

DESSERT

RUSTIC STRAWBERRY TART

You'll need 3-4 punnets of fresh strawberries for this easy summer tart. Work quickly and carefully when rolling and folding the pastry as it will be soft. Gently press any small cracks back together. Serve the pie with vanilla ice cream, fresh cream or thick Greek yoghurt.

SERVES 8-10

500 g (1 lb 2 oz) sweet short pastry (I use Paneton)
700 g (1 lb 9 oz) strawberries
2 tablespoons caster sugar (plus extra to sprinkle)
2 teaspoons cornflour
½ teaspoon vanilla paste or essence
1 egg – whisked
2 tablespoons strawberry jam (optional for glazing)

Preheat the oven to 180°C (350°F) fan bake.

Line a baking tray with baking paper.

Roll out the pastry to roughly 40 x 30 cm (16 x 12 in) on the lined baking tray.

Hull the strawberries, then slice them into quarters. Place in a bowl with the sugar, cornflour and vanilla and mix gently.

Arrange the strawberries in the middle of the pastry, leaving a 5 cm (2 in) border around the edges. Brush the border of the pastry with the egg wash.

Fold up the edges of the pastry around the strawberries and gently pinch together to create a very rough crust, leaving the middle exposed.

Brush the outer edges with the egg wash and gently sprinkle the extra sugar around the crust. Bake for roughly 45–50 minutes or until the base is golden in colour.

Leave on the tray to cool for 10 minutes before serving. If desired, gently brush the jam over the strawberries to glaze.

FLOURLESS HAZELNUT BROWNIE CAKE

This reminds me of a Ferrero Rocher chocolate, ie HEAVEN, like a slightly nutty brownie/cake hybrid. The compote is a welcome addition, as is a dollop of thick Greek yoghurt to serve. Hazelnut flour is also called hazelnut meal. If you can't find it, blend two cups of skinless hazelnuts into flour.

SERVES 8

120 g (4¼ oz) butter
250 g (9 oz) dark chocolate – chopped
¾ cup soft brown sugar
3 large eggs – at room temperature
½ teaspoon vanilla paste
2 cups hazelnut flour
½ teaspoon baking powder
¼ cup cocoa powder

BERRY COMPOTE

2 cups frozen mixed berries
2 tablespoons caster sugar (or more, to taste)

Preheat the oven to 160°C (315°F) fan bake.

Grease a 20 cm (8 in) springform cake tin with butter.

Melt the butter and chocolate in a large bowl in the microwave until nice and smooth. Do this in short bursts, giving it a good stir in between.

Whisk in the sugar. Add the eggs one by one, whisking in between. Add the vanilla, whisking well until everything is combined.

Add the hazelnut flour and baking powder, then sieve in the cocoa powder. Stir until just combined but don't over-stir.

Pour the mixture into the cake tin and bake for 45 minutes. The top should have a slight crust.

Let the cake cool in the tin for 15 minutes, then very carefully remove the sides and lift it off the base, placing it on a wire rack to cool completely.

To make the Berry Compote, warm the berries in a medium saucepan on a medium heat until defrosted. Add the sugar, stir until dissolved, then remove from the heat. Serve with the cooled cake.

BANOFFEE PIE

Banoffee Pie is one of my favourite desserts, on par with about ten others, haha! In my eyes, the double layer of bananas is a very welcome addition. If you aren't eating this straight away, you need to keep it in the fridge until serving.

SERVES 10

400 g (14 oz) chocolate
   digestive biscuits
150 g (5½ oz) unsalted
   butter – melted
4 large bananas
395 g (14 oz) can ready-to-use
   caramel
300 ml (10½ fl oz) cream
Dark chocolate – grated or
   flaked

Using a food processor, blitz the biscuits into a crumb. Pour in the melted butter and whizz until very well combined.

Pour the crumb into a 25 cm (10 in) quiche tin with a removable base and press down firmly so it is evenly spread across the base and sides of the tin.

Put in the freezer to chill for half an hour (it needs to be nice and firm).

Slice 2 of the bananas into 5 mm (¼ in) rounds. Arrange over the base, overlapping, until the base is covered.

Spread the caramel evenly over the top of the bananas.

Slice the remaining 2 bananas into rounds and add a second layer on top of the caramel.

Whip the cream and spread it over the bananas.

Garnish with lots of grated or flaked chocolate. Carefully remove the sides of the tin and serve immediately while it's cold!

Acknowledgements

Firstly, to my parents: Kim and my late papa, Les. Thank you for your unconditional love, support and constant encouragement, which made me believe I can do everything and anything I put my mind to.

My beautiful sister, Lucy: you tested more recipes for me than I could count. Thanks for giving me constant feedback on my choice of flavours and cook times and my never-ending grammatical errors (Dad would've been impressed).

My darling brother, Jack: your love of food - or eating, should I say - is up there with mine. Thanks for being the most enthusiastic sampler and for always being in my corner.

Felix, the chief of all taste testers! Thank you for your honest and hilarious reviews of my cooking, for never ever letting me do the constant stream of dishes, and for being the biggest support among the madness.

Jo and Mel - the dream team. I had the best few weeks working with you both and I will treasure those memories forever. I can't wait to do it all over again sometime soon!

Lynley - the queen of sweet foods. Thank you for helping me and for critiquing my desserts. You are an angel.

Madeline and Margie - the best in the business. Thank you for editing and rewording some of my outrageously terrible attempts at writing pitches for Allen & Unwin.

Millie, Ollie and Coco, thank you so much for letting me take over your beautiful home for the cover shoot. Thanks also to Harris Tapper for the gorgeous clothes you dressed me in for some of the shots, and to French Country Collections for your divine platters, cutlery and plates.

Thanks to Michelle and the team at Allen & Unwin for approaching me in the first place to write this book, and for your help in putting it all together.

And finally, to all my special friends who played a part in the making of this book (recipe testing, eating and listening to me go on and on about cooking), thank you for never letting me give up.

I couldn't have done this book without you all.

Love, Polly xx

Index

Note: Polly uses New Zealand standard measures, including the 15 ml (3 teaspoon) tablespoon. If you are using the Australian 20 ml (4 teaspoon) tablespoon, you may wish to remove a teaspoon of ingredient for each tablespoon specified.

First published in 2022
Text © Polly Markus, 2022
Photography © Melanie Jenkins (Flash Studios), 2022
Styling by Jo Bridgford (Delivision Food Styling)

Allen & Unwin
Level 2, 10 College Hill, Freemans Bay
Auckland 1011, New Zealand
Phone: (64 9) 377 3800
Email: auckland@allenandunwin.com
Web: www.allenandunwin.co.nz

83 Alexander Street
Crows Nest NSW 2065, Australia
Phone: (61 2) 8425 0100

A catalogue record for this book is available from the National Library of New Zealand.

ISBN 978 1 98854 797 8

Design by Megan van Staden
Set in Galaxie Copernicus and National

Printed in China by C & C Offset Printing Co. Ltd

1 3 5 7 9 10 8 6 4 2